Imagery in the Novels of André Malraux

Imagery in the Novels of André Malraux

Ralph Tarica

Rutherford • Madison • Teaneck
Fairleigh Dickinson University Press
London and Toronto: Associated University Presses

©1980 by Associated University Presses, Inc.

Associated University Presses, Inc.
Cranbury, New Jersey 08512

Associated University Presses
Magdalen House
136-148 Tooley Street
London SE1 2TT, England

Associated University Presses
Toronto M5E 1A7, Canada

Library of Congress Cataloging in Publication Data

Tarica, Ralph, 1932-
Imagery in the novels of André Malraux.
Bibliography: p.
Includes index.
1. Malraux, André, 1901-1976—Style. 2. Figures of speech. I. Title.
PQ2625.A716Z9434 843'.9'12 78-75189
ISBN 0-8386-2269-0

Printed in the United States of America

To Suzanne

Contents

List of Abbreviations

All page references to Malraux's work are taken from the French editions (for complete data the Bibliography should be consulted). What is metaphorical in one language may often turn out to be merely clumsy in another. I have therefore translated Malraux's texts into English myself in an effort to preserve the metaphorical quality of the original French, which has frequently been lost in the standard available translations. My translations have admittedly lost in smoothness of English expression what they have gained in preciseness of image identity.

LC *Les Conquérants*

VR *La Voie Royale*

CH *La Condition humaine*

TM *Le Temps du mépris*

LE *L'Espoir*

NA *Les Noyers de l'Altenburg*

Acknowledgments

I wish to thank the following publishers for having given me permission to quote or to translate excerpts from the works of André Malraux.

Editions Gallimard: *La Condition humaine*, copyright 1933; *L'Espoir*, copyright 1937; *Les Noyers de l'Altenburg*, copyright 1948.

Editions Bernard Grasset: *La Voie Royale*, copyright 1930; *Les Conquérants*, copyright 1928.

Victor Gollancz Ltd.: *Days of Contempt*, translated by Haakon M. Chevalier, copyright 1936.

Hamish Hamilton Ltd.: *Man's Estate*, translated by Alastair MacDonald, copyright 1934; *Man's Hope*, translated by Stuart Gilbert and Alastair MacDonald, copyright 1938.

Random House, Inc.: *Man's Fate*, translated by Haakon M. Chevalier, copyright 1934; *The Royal Way*, translated by Stuart Gilbert, copyright 1935; *Days of Wrath*, translated by Haakon M. Chevalier, copyright 1936; *Man's Hope*, translated by Stuart Gilbert and Alastair MacDonald, copyright 1938.

I am grateful to Harvard University for permission to use portions of a chapter previously published in *Image and Theme: Studies in Modern French Fiction*, pp. 38-73 (Copyright 1969 by the President and Fellows of Harvard College), and to The Malraux Society for material in *Mélanges Malraux Miscellany*, Vol. X, no. 2, pp. 3-11 (Copyright 1978 by Walter G. Langlois, Editor).

Finally, I would particularly like to express my thanks

to the General Research Board of the University of Maryland for the financial support that allowed me to prepare this study for publication.

Introduction

The novels of André Malraux carry heavy burdens. They are the records of an intellectual deeply committed to exploring questions that have perhaps always beset the humanist, and of an adventurer who has sought the answers through action as well as thought. Psychological investigation, metaphysical speculation, political commentary and even propaganda—these make up the enterprise of a writer who is rightly considered a witness of our era and of its struggles.

Yet Malraux in his novels is not only a witness but a writer, too—an artist who has imposed the order of creative imagination upon personal thought and experience. It is to that creative imagination that this study directs the reader's attention, through a focus on the imagery in the six novels of Malraux and their relationship to motif, theme, style and structure in these works.

Two major assumptions underlie the efforts represented in this study. One has to do with the value of carrying on image studies as a significant form of literary criticism. Metaphorical language has long been recognized as being uniquely suited for setting up complex relationships between the various components of the world depicted by the writer. The image informs us in a subtle, oblique manner of something the writer wishes to express—indeed, may be obliged to express—in subliminal relationship to the story line. The impact upon the reader can be seen as a momentary state of perception, suspended somewhere between a purely subjective, incommunicable truth and a purely objective, discursive one. Being essentially a poetic insight it is at the heart of the creative imagination, and by its very nature will always retain an elusive quality. Indeed, the degree to which it is felt as an image at all will depend upon the intelligence, sensitivity and, perhaps ultimately, upon the sheer receptivity of the reader.

Yet a consideration of a novelist's imagery is not beyond objective analysis. Though the image has a subtle, complex structure, at its core lies an analogy of some sort, drawn from the world of communicable reality, and a manner of expression having its particular characteristic form; and whatever the structure, the image performs a characteristic function. This reality, this form, and this function may be profitably studied.

The second assumption is that the novels of André Malraux, having now reached the point in time where they constitute something of a classical canon and showing every sign of remaining one of the major bodies of fiction in modern French literature, are deserving of a total image study. There is, of course, no lack of excellent critical literature on Malraux's novels that focus on thematic content. Works according generous consideration to Malraux's style and imagery have appeared more rarely, although in recent years their number has grown fairly considerably. In all the full-length books concerned with the imagery, however, the concern is subordinated to a more predominant line of interest, as usually revealed in the subtitles (for example, "The Conquest of Dread," "The Human Adventure," "The Metamorphosis of Death").[1] The most systematic study of Malraux's fictional techniques in recent years is probably Jean Carduner's *La Création romanesque chez Malraux* (Paris, 1968), but even Carduner admits: "L'étude de l'imaginaire chez Malraux reste à faire" (p. 13), while he none the less contributes immeasurably to attaining that goal in his own work.

I am indebted to these and many other critics for a number of insights from which this study has benefited. For the most part, however, I have allowed my material to speak for itself. By this I mean, firstly, that this study has taken into account all of the imagery in all six of Malraux's novels, and has exploited as fully as possible comparisons and analyses based on the widest possible body of material. Oversights have no doubt been inevitable, despite several close readings of the texts accompanied by a careful gleaning of all significant material; and for this I ask the reader's indulgence beforehand. Secondly, this study has been undertaken with no *a priori* thesis in mind, but with a view to allowing the material to suggest its own patterns of expressive function and thematic meaning. Here again omissions are unavoidable. It goes without saying that all the possible meanings contained in a large and complex body of imagery can never be entirely deduced. My development of Malraux's image patterns must be viewed as a partial or simply introductory treatment of a complex topic. Beyond that, I can only hope that, despite lengthy reflection on the material under consideration, none of the major patterns have been overlooked.

Given the sustained interest in Malraux's work throughout the world today, it is my hope that this study will find its justification if it has provided new insights into the creative imagination of one of the great writers of our times; and, above all, if it provides the student of Malraux with the necessary materials with which to pursue paths leading to still further insight and to work that may still profitably be done.

Notes

1. See Gerda Blumenthal, *André Malraux: The Conquest of Dread* (Baltimore, Md.: Johns Hopkins University Press, 1960); Violet M. Horvath, *André Malraux: The Human Adventure* (New York: New York University Press, 1969); Thomas J. Kline, *André Malraux and the Metamorphosis of Death* (New York: Columbia University Press, 1973).

Imagery in the Novels of André Malraux

[1]

Malraux's World of Images

A reader need consider no more than a few pages chosen at random from Malraux's novels to be impressed with the number and density of images. A more careful reading of the novels will prove that this metaphorical language is particularly suited to help the novels carry their discursive burdens. It is probably no exaggeration to say that Malraux's reader need not be endowed with a superior sensibility to be affected by the quality of the imagery: anyone who has read a novel of Malraux's is likely to have been struck by the "gripping" quality of the text. This goes a long way towards explaining one of the important functions of the imagery. All of the quasi-analogical structures—elements in decor which combine to form dense and brooding atmospheres, the intrusions upon plot and thought by exterior presences—and a greater number of the purely analogical images are woven inextricably into the narrative in such a way as to magnetize us onto an experience, and through vivid dramatic highlighting and blowups, make that experience ours.

However, before attempting to understand the quality of Malraux's imagery we must first determine more precisely what material we shall be dealing with and what we can reasonably hope to gain from studying it.

Image Sources

At the heart of any metaphorical system lies a process of analogy-making, involving the elaboration of a literal sign by another nonliteral element on the basis of some quality shared by both—what I. A. Richards has henceforth consecrated in critical language as the "tenor," the "vehicle," and the "ground" of the image.

The "vehicles," or sources, of Malraux's imagery are drawn from realms of experience which can be shared by both author and reader—not so much because we have done similar things (if we recall, some of Malraux's exploits have become legendary), but because we understand a common language. Even if we grant that an author's images originate in the closed world of the subjective imagination, on the printed page they none the less become objective data which can be studied to understand more fully what the author is saying. A consideration of the image sources in all the novels—especially the images that recur with some frequency—permits us to map out and explore a consistent phenomenological frame of reference, what one might consider the unified landscape of the author's imagination.

A study of the relationship between tenor and vehicle can lead us to a closer perception of the author's psychological and poetic confrontation with reality. Exploring the "ground" of the image—the element which presumably induced the writer's imagination to create an analogy in the first place—is tantamount to a study of the author's themes.[1] It may indeed be the most productive way of studying those themes, since its formal, intrinsic approach may allow for a more objective manner of handling the complete body of the writer's material than an approach based on such extrinsic categories as love, death, solitude, politics, art history, and so forth. These are among the more obvious benefits that can result from an image study such as proposed here.

The first task of a work such as this must be to amass relevant data. Subsequently the data must be ordered according to some system of categories, and then sifted for patterns of significance. The chapters that follow may be seen, at their most fundamental level, as a *description* of the resulting material: Malraux's significant imagery, grouped in clusters of logically related elements. To arrive at the significant imagery, I have initially considered as worthy of study *all* of Malraux's imagery—metaphors, similes, personifications, metonymies, and recurrent motifs having internally consistent references, whether strikingly original as expressive figures or as outmoded as the dullest cliches—in order to exploit as wide a scope of literary devices as possible, before detecting those elements which provide the surest keys for understanding the novels. The study has been ordered, for practical purposes, according to the traditional sequence that begins with inanimate nature continuing through vegetation, animals, human beings, and human activities and experiences. This arrangement, in fact, proves to go beyond the merely practical in that it reveals in its own right certain broad patterns of stylistic characteristics and thematic meaning. Recent notions on structural paradigms have served this work as a useful corrective device for the double hazard of rigidity of classification and deceptive simplification. I have not associated the image of the moon and planets, for example, with such elements as the sun, light, clouds, and so forth, to which they may be logically related from a phenomenal point of view, but rather to a quite special group of vehicles which Malraux consistently draws upon to communicate a feeling of strangeness and unreality.

What therefore appeared to be fundamentally a work of description turns out inevitably to be an interpretative attempt to establish objective patterns at a number of levels, through exploring the central creative consciousness which produced (for purposes of this study, at least) six works of fiction dating from the late 1920s to the early 1940s. The aim here is obviously not to reconstruct the author's biography on the basis of his choice of images; an author's creative imagination and his biography are not of the same order of experience. Neither is it "to divert attention from the novels as individual works of art and to focus it on them as materials for the study of the creative mind," a serious hazard of image studies pointed out by W. M. Frohock.[2] What is involved is a double process of induction and deduction. By amassing and comparing a large number of particular examples, each of which reveals relatively little in itself, general patterns of meaning are revealed which can then be employed to inform the particular examples. From the text we move towards an "ideal" creative imagination, and then return to the text with the tools with which to understand it better.[3] There is admittedly a hazard in viewing an author's creative potential as a solid block of consistent imaginative processes unchanging over the course of his productive life. But in fact much of Malraux's choice and use of imagery does tend to be consistent from the first to the last of his novels (and even, as it would not be difficult to demonstrate, from his earliest fictional work of the mid-1920s to his most recent books of the 1960s and 1970s). As for the inconsistencies that do exist, one of the goals of this work will be to point out some of the more obvious modifications that can be detected when looking at Malraux's novels in chronological sequence.

Finally, I have throughout this work made a conscious effort not to consider the images as abstract phenomena, but have tried to relate them within as full a context as possible, taking into account the full range of the narrator's perception as expressed through the narrator's rhetoric, including visual and atmospheric composition, dynamic modulations such as ellipsis and recurrence of motif, as well as thematic significance.

Image Forms

Malraux's style is marked by a persistent tendency to establish multiple correspondencies, even at a virtually literal level where it would be difficult to speak in terms of traditional image forms. Linking words such as "lié à" (bound to), and "s'accorder à," "être d'accord avec" (to match, to suit, or to be in harmony with, but where the musical connotation is clearly missing) quite literally abound in all the novels, constituting a loosely metonymic kind of image: that is, two separate and normally unrelated elements are brought into figurative union through an expressed contiguity. Towards the end of *La Voie Royale*, for example, we read that the howling of wild dogs "were in harmony with" Perken's ravaged face (VR, p. 263); and in *L'Espoir,* Sembrano's sad smile is "in tune with" approaching night (LE, p. 501). The correspondence is thus established on the basis of some aspect of phenomenological reality and the psychological state of a character, usually an anxious one.

Similarly, a whole atmosphere may take on sympathetic movement through Malraux's expression of a "rhythm"; and again, the effect is almost always associated with a sense of anxiety. The accompaniment may consist of noises. We read, for example: "A calm filled with anxiety. The rhythmic sound, becoming increasingly clear, of the marching of approaching men" (LC, p. 88). It may consist of battle reverberations: glasses filled with drinks "quivered to the rhythm of the fighting. The soldier drank. Slowly his breathing came back to normal" (LE, p. 463). We find it most often related to a pulsating of the blood or to breathing patterns: Perken's advance through the jungle is rapid, but its "rhythm" is set by the beating of blood in his wounded leg (VR, p. 316). In a slightly more subtle variation, we find numerous instances where light falls upon men and objects, creating an effect of depth through the reflection of one thing in another. And again, in virtually every instance, the effect is related to a feeling of uneasiness. As Tchen discusses terrorism with his two accomplices, the reflections on the bowls of nearby lamps suddenly and mysteriously disappear (CH, p. 315). During the Toledo episode of *L'Espoir,* the delirious gestures of plaster saints "reflected the bluish peace of the evening" (LE, p. 580). During a tank episode we read that "the thing that has been lighting up our faces drained of life is the mirror reflecting the moonlit sky" (NA, p. 279).

Malraux employs a wide gamut of expressions to "thicken" an atmosphere through the illusion of substantive weight and depth: "filled with" (plein de, empli de, rempli de), "studded with" (criblé de), "in a" (dans un), "beneath" (sous), "in the depth of" (au fond de), "with" (avec, mêlé avec), and several other prepositional linking words through which Malraux achieves a vivid, sensuous quality. For example: "this silence is filled with arms" (LC, p. 39), "the silence remained suspended, filled with the gear noises of the truck" (LE, p. 684), a "cavalry slipped by in the depth of night" (NA, p. 181), "savagery with its smell of meat" (VR, p. 149). The device which will probably be most familiar to Malraux readers as a stylistic hallmark is the expression "to fade away into" (se perdre dans) which might well be associated with Malraux's interest in cinematic technique: "the line of shadow—disturbed by slow movements which fade into it" (LC, p. 88); "the enormous characters faded into this hazy, tragic world" (CH, p. 353); "the Romanesque arches in the shadows, into which the shelves of books faded away" (NA, p. 83), etc.

All of these loosely figurative expressions, aside from underscoring what amounts to a conspiracy between the universe and the nerves, emotions, and thoughts of Malraux's characters, may be seen as part of the author's rather considerable stock of devices for creating dramatic effects—or, to be more to the point, for dramatizing experience in the context of anxiety. They are amplifying tools for controlling the dynamic movement of a passage, modulating the intensity of our perceptions from a crescendo to a diminuendo, or vice versa, in fairly rapid order. They are indicative, in general, of the author's tendency towards hyperbolic expression of a romantic sort—a tendency which is further borne out when we consider Malraux's use of more fixed image forms.

Metonymy—more specifically, that kind of metonymy usually referred to as synecdoche, in which the whole is represented by one of its parts—is a recurrent Malraux device for creating a certain type of dramatic effect. The narrating voice frequently reduces persons and objects to vague shapes looming darkly over an action: "human shadows moved beneath the dim lightbulbs" (CH, p. 371); it can focus our attention, dramatically, on an act of great significance: Katow bestows the greatest gift of life—paradoxically, a capsule of poison—upon a "warm hand which was touching him, not even to bodies, not even to voices" (CH, p. 409) so that the entire weight of the fraternal theme is borne by the hand alone.

Personification and animation are related figurative forms which appear with considerable frequency in all the novels. Malraux transposes aspects of human biology, society, sentiment, thought, attitude and movement from the human to the non-human sphere, to render his universe alternately sympathetic, hostile or indifferent to the plight of man. He applies animal characteristics, or simply some aspect of any living being, to inanimate entities—Malraux does not seem to be so much interested in personifying the universe as he is in suffusing it with life. Personification and animation may thus relate to objects: trucks lie on their backs, their "paws" in the air (LE, p. 518); to atmospheric presences: a fresh wind blows "faithfully" towards Russia (NA, p. 181); even to abstractions—there are a dozen or so simple allegories of the sort in which music cradles Kassner's head between her "hands" (TM, p. 51).

Malraux's inclination for projecting life upon matter—

especially in cases where an individual finds himself confronted by a universe reflecting every thought and sensation running through mind and body—might well be considered "romantic." But it would be more to the point if we think of these interchanges of life forces among human, animate and inanimate bodies as a predominant characteristic of the author's mythic vision of reality. In his preface to *Le Temps du mépris* Malraux explains that the hero in this book (but the message applies really to all his books) confronts not the world but his sense of life (p. 8). In this confrontation, the objects, entities and ideas that make up the world can take on a vital energy that transforms them from mere matter and thought into a character with its own role to play along with the heroes.

The simile set up by the traditional *comme* is the most frequent image form in Malraux, though there is an abundance of other recurrent types of explicit comparisons. The most frequent linking words are *en:* roofing tiles explode like a geyser, "en geyser" (LE, p. 521); *de:* a Last Judgment night, "nuit de dernier jugement" (CH, p. 193); *à aspect de:* an old man looking like a bewildered clergyman, "à aspect de clergyman ahuri" (CH, p. 196); *l'air de:* a character looks somewhat like a vampire, "son petit air de vampire" (NA, p. 129).

What might strike one as curious is that in an author whose style is so frequently elliptical, the simile should appear considerably more often than the metaphor—that is, the expanded, explicit form predominates over the elliptical, implicit form. Stephen Ullmann may provide us with a key for understanding this apparent paradox when he points out that the simile may express a naive, unsophisticated, pseudoepic intent, while the metaphor seeks an effect of surprise and shock.[4] The lesson applies well in Malraux's case. Malraux's vision is essentially that of the innocent exposed to the horrors of living, physical and metaphysical—or rather, who repeatedly exposes himself to those horrors, since six novels would surely be sufficient evidence to indicate a fatal fascination for the predicaments against which his characters struggle. Malraux is not so much interested in shocking the reader as he is in informing him of the shock his characters experience upon engagement with reality. Each new confrontation invites a new discovery, a new impression, a new engagement, a new simile—and the preponderent number of these similes reveals how often those confrontations take place.

The expressive range of Malraux's similes and their capacity for originality remains wide; the metaphor is restricted to relatively few tasks. First, it is employed to designate an entity which has already been expressed as a simile. Towards the end of *La Voie Royale*, for example, we read that smoke rising from the fires made by jungle tribesmen "closed the horizon like enormous bars"; shortly afterwards we read that Perken's sufferings merged "with these bars of smoke" (VR, pp. 261-62). The simile thus *creates* the experience, engages the character, and us, in his fate, while the metaphor merely repeats the result. Secondly, the metaphor tends to apply to rather commonplace substantive expressions, such as a "cluster" of hopes, the noonday "furnace" (VR, p. 261), and to a fairly large number of adjectival clichés: "a stagnant world" (VR, pp. 54-55), "faces leaden-hued with hunger" (NA, p. 19). Thirdly, it often appears in passages where important and dramatic action is halted so that the narrating voice can make grave (and occasionally somewhat melodramatic) pronouncements. As Kyo sits next to Katow, before dying, he thinks of Katow as a "condemned life, shipwrecked next to his own in the shadows filled with menace and wounds, among all these brothers in the mendicant order of the Revolution" (CH, p. 403). Bonneau, caught in a tank trap and, through sheer terror, opening and closing his tank door, "beats the sinister tom-tom of delirium" (NA, p. 275).

There is a particularly abundant group of verbal analogies established through as-if types of statements, clauses beginning with *comme si, comme pour, comme lorsque, sembler que, on dirait que*, etc. (I have noted over a hundred instances in *La Condition humaine* alone). They may serve the narrating voice in modulating perceptions: "as if the darkness had made the fog thicker, a locomotive siren sounded from far off" (CH, p. 402). They may establish a physical description in company with vocal expression: "König's index finger moved as though he had continued to speak" (CH, p. 378). These constructions often give solid support to an important theme in Malraux, the primacy of action over speech, the replacement of words by gesture for effective communication. Clappique, who never seems to be at a loss for words normally, cannot find them in one of his few moments of despair: "as though the anxiety which could not be translated into words had been expressed directly in all their power, he began to make faces" (CH, p. 372); and even in the case of Gisors, who is not notable for his desire for action, we learn that his gestures, when prolonging a statement, "did not seem to brush something aside, but rather to grasp something" (CH, p. 209).

This type of construction in Malraux can usually be seen as a device for setting up a close bond between two elements: between a person and a mannerism that characterizes him, between human thought or emotions and inanimate entities, between an inanimate entity and an abstract quality projected upon it; examples abound in all Malraux's novels. But it is worth noting that in a number of cases what is depicted is the psychological impression of a situation felt as paradoxical or contrary to fact. A feeling of bewilderment may thus underscore a character's sense of solitude. Before Tchen kills his first victim, for example, he stuffs his hands deep into his pocket "as though the night were not enough to hide his gestures" (CH, p. 182), and raises his right arm, "stupefied by the silence which continued to surround him, as though his movement should have caused something to fall" (CH, p. 182).

Image Density

Within each novel, needless to say, there are considerable variations in metaphorical density from one episode to the next.[5] The unelaborated extreme (the "blank" style) tends to occur in certain passages of expository background information—plans for battle, for example, and descriptions of an overall political situation—but even here it is rare that Malraux can write for more than a page or two without eventually resorting to an image. The other extreme occurs at those moments of revelation in which a hero's understanding of events suddenly bursts into a flood of image-making. Between the two extremes fluctuations range from the relatively blank passages of philosophical discourse, in which major themes are elaborated primarily through reflection and dialogue, to the relatively fertile descriptions of mass activities in city streets and on the battlefield.

In *Les Conquérants* the extreme densities occur most often in connection with descriptions of Chinese street scenes—the sight of extreme poverty mixed with exotic, fascinating colors (in particular during Tcheng-Dai's funeral) seems to provoke a sense of wonder in the narrator's mind and eye. In *La Voie Royale* two major explosions occur, one during the climactic confrontation between the European explorers and the jungle tribesmen, and another in the final episode where Perken's sense of disintegration becomes a blinding revelation (there are close to forty images in the five pages that begin with page 261).

In *La Condition humaine* there is an abundance of revelations and an equal abundance of dense passages, beginning with the very first scene, in which Tchen discovers the world of the murderer, to the last opium dream of Gisors. Two relatively blank episodes are worthy of note, one in which Malraux describes Tchen's visit to an antique shop as part of his scenario to assassinate Chiang Kai-shek (about four images in four pages) and the other depicting Ferral's final predicament in Paris (about ten images in a little over eleven pages). In the first, the terseness of the sentence structure and the absence of many figures holds activity in suspense, shifting the focus on Tchen's nervous anxiety away from psychological introspection (what we usually expect in this novel) to purely exterior events. In the second, the scarcity of images accentuates the purely discursive language of the highly placed bureaucrats with whom Ferral must deal. At one point, they all begin chewing candy, so that the two acts, discursive speech and chewing, become a single gesture of meaninglessness for Ferral, conveying the ironic fate that has befallen this man of will and action.

In *Le Temps du mépris* we are faced with a considerable body of image-making during Kassner's stay in prison—but image-making of a rather special kind. A great deal of what passes through Kassner's mind is picture memories and a wild sort of daydreaming not unlike Gisors's first opium dream (CH, pp. 229-30). We are dealing here with a kind of proto-imagery, a body of impressions that rush through the mind, out of control and *without form*—one impression suddenly congeals into another, but the expression is often not even metaphoric. This lack of form suggests a return to a primitive state, the loss of lucid vision; and it is significant that when the pictures do take on a form, especially that of the simile, we know that Kassner is in control again, if only for a moment.

In *L'Espoir* the great spurts of imagery apply most often to the nonhuman. More than ever, the elements—clouds, fires, the earth, the sea—seem to be flooded with a life that endows human activity with mythic and epic proportions; or else, by the sheer contrast of density and paucity of imagery, they belie the acts of man. *Les Noyers de l'Altenburg* has three episodes that explode with imagery, and they are all associated with the revelation that comes through a consideration of human activity against the backdrop of nature: Vincent Berger's contemplation of the walnut trees, his wonder at the rebirth of life in a field destroyed by poison gas, and the narrator's prolonged sense of personal rebirth during the final five or six pages of the novel.

Image Development

Once Malraux has noted the figurative relationship between two entities he generally likes to develop it in one way or another—the single vehicle that appears only once is relatively rare. The elaboration of the image can follow a variety of patterns. The simplest is that of the repetition of the same image to apply to the same object; having decided that Clappique's voice belongs to a punchinello in one simile (CH, p. 196) Malraux will apply the figure to Clappique in the form of a metaphor four more times in the following pages. This movement from the simple simile to the simple metaphor in Malraux's depiction of character appears particularly often as a derogatory device: Kassner's guards are "overcoats" (TM, p. 114) and "walruses" (TM, p. 115), Chpilewski an "eagle" (CH, p. 297).

A more complex pattern is the image that becomes a rhythm by relating to its object several times during the course of the novel. Leclerc is seen "sitting like a monkey" (LE, p. 476), and subsequently as "a skinny monkey in overalls," a "big monkey with clownish wisps of hair" and so on through two more images (LE, pp. 479, 671, 678, 684). In many cases, this sort of rhythm takes on its cumulative effect on the basis of several vaguely related vehicles: Clappique looks pitiably like a good dog (CH, p. 201), has the face of a "sad and chilly monkey" (CH, p. 320); then, standing before his mirror grimacing at himself, he transforms himself, in rapid succession, into a "gargoyle," a "carnival samorai," a "monkey," an "idiot," and a "toad-face" (CH, pp. 372-73). There are a few instances of associations that develop into a rhythm through several novels, so that the image turns into a constant correlative: passing clouds connote ephemeral lives, stars signify fate, insects flying about a light become men moving towards their death, and so on. In such cases of strictly assigned meanings we can speak of symbols, and the mere presence of clouds, stars, or insects flying about a light delivers its message without recourse to analogical form.

Another frequent pattern is the elaboration of an image sequence applied to the same object. The sequence may belong to the same category of experience. The following image, for example, describes Attignies's mental state as he crouches with war refugees in a tunnel: "everything that had been previously life became diluted like paltry memories in a deep and gloomy torpor; the specks of light in this hot darkness were leading their lives like fish in great ocean depressions, and the political commissar [Attignies] slipped motionlessly and weightlessly far beyond death, through a great river of sleep" (LE, p. 797). Here the images of dilution, fish swimming at great depth, weightlessness, all have to do with water and floating, and they depict a state of mental energy falling at a rapid pace; the next image shifts figurative direction from sea depth to that of a river, underground because the sleep takes place in a tunnel, while the whole sequence suggests a traditional descent into hell.

In this particular instance the images move towards a climactic dream-death, but more often patterns of this sort move dramatically towards an exhilarating feeling of awareness. The narrator of *Les Noyers de l'Altenburg,* having recently escaped from a tank trap, comes upon a farmyard and reflects: "I still bear within me the irruption of earthly night that I felt upon coming out of the pit, that germination in the darkness heightened by constellations in the holes of floating clouds; and just as this rumbling, full night arose from the pit, now out of the night arises the miraculous revelation of day" (NA, pp. 289-90). Here the sequence of birth images applies first to night, then to day, and by sheer dramatic thrust, to the speaker himself.

Some of these elaborate sequences focus vehicles from unrelated fields on a single object. The narrator of *Les Conquérants* finds in Klein's physique "something of a boxer, a bulldog and a butcher" (LC, p. 36). More prolonged developments appear with considerable frequency, projecting multiple perspectives on the same subject. Clappique grimacing at his mirror provides one good example. Another occurs where Claude Vannec, after spending an enormous amount of energy trying to crack a stone sculpture, looks at the result: "In the triangular slit, the dust of the stone flowed slowly, shining and white as salt, accentuating through its hourglass fall the mass of the stone, the stone which was now taking on again an indestructible life, a mountainlike life: his stare remained its prisoner. He felt tied to it through hatred as though to an animate being" (VR, p. 124). Here we have literally a stone and Claude, but the sequence of images directs our attention to their relationship, progressing from the futility of Claude's efforts to master the stone to the realization that the stone has mastered Claude.

There are, finally, image sequences that set up a dense body of intertwined associations tending to resist logical unraveling. Far from being exceptional, they are rather a hallmark of Malraux's style. A good example occurs towards the end of *La Voie Royale*. Perken, accompanied by his young friend and accomplice Claude, has reached the end of his rope. In the course of his jungle adventure he has experienced both victory and defeat: victory in that he has secured the ancient Khmer sculptures, the sale of which will guarantee his wealth and his continued rule over his jungle vassals; defeat in that he has discovered that other great white hunter, Grabot, in a state of total and humiliating ruin. Finally, as he heads back towards his jungle empire which is about to be invaded by railroad construction crews, he experiences a profound sense of frustration:

> . . . he understood simultaneously that he would get well at home, and that he would die, that the world would close over the cluster of hopes that he had become, bound by this railway as though by a prisoner's rope; that nothing in the universe, not ever, could compensate for his past sufferings or his present sufferings: to be a man was even more absurd than to die . . . . Becoming more and more numerous now, enormous and rising vertically in the noonday furnace, the smoke of the Mei fires closed off the horizon like gigantic bars: the heat, his fever, the cart, his burns, the barking of the dogs, these railroad ties thrown down like shovels full of earth over his body, merged with these bars of smoke and the power of the jungle, with death itself, in a superhuman, hopeless imprisonment. (VR, pp. 261-62)

There seems to be little apparent relation between a world that closes over a man's hopes and a world bound tight by a railway. We are dealing here with a kind of perceptual movement frequent in Malraux: a situation is perceived by the intelligence as a predicament, awareness of the predicament then induces a sense of anxiety that exteriorizes itself by projection upon the original situation. Perken's anguish here projects itself along two lines of reference, both having to do with enclosing. In one, he feels that he and his hopes are being covered up by a hostile world represented by the railway. This feeling repeats itself in the image of the railwayties, and here again the image seems rather farfetched: there is no real connection between laying ties on a track and shoveling earth on a corpse. But the interior, psychological logic is there: the presence of a railway means the death of Perken. In the other line of reference, Perken finds that the railway is binding his world just as a rope binds a prisoner. In this case the feeling of imprisonment is pursued through the image of smoke and bars, further elaborated to lead to an overwhelming sense of a superhuman, hopeless imprisonment.

Image and Narrating Voice

A final word is necessary to understand the relationship between Malraux's images, his characters, and the narrating voice. What Malraux directs the reader to perceive generally bears directly on the experience of at least one of the characters in an episode, but may not necessarily be reported through the eyes or senses of the character himself. In *La Voie Royale*, for example, Claude Vannec wonders whether or not his party can penetrate the heavy jungle to discover the lost statues: "Clear a road through such vegetation? Others had done it, therefore he could do it. To this uneasy affirmation the overcast sky and the inextricable matting of leaves riddled with insects opposed their silent affirmation" (VR, p. 57). This somewhat heavy intrusion into Claude's thought by the narrating voice serves to inform the reader of trouble ahead, and engages him in the adventure to come. In another instance, in *La Condition humaine*, Kyo and Katow make their rounds of the revolutionary cells in Shanghai, and come to a shop in the pet merchants' quarter: "After knocking they entered one of the shops: that of a pet fish dealer. The only light, a candle stuck into a lantern, was reflected by a row of phosphorescent jars, aligned like those of Ali Baba, and in which were sleeping, invisible, the renowned carps of China." The merchant-agent reports that a general strike is set for noon the next day, and without any transition Malraux writes: "Without anything changing in the shadows, without a gesture from the merchant drowsing at the back of his nook, the phosphorescent surface of all the jars began to stir slightly; soft black concentric waves arose silently: the sound of the voices had awakened the fish. Another siren faded into the distance" (CH, pp. 206-7).

Again, it would seem to be the reader, and not the

characters, who is forewarned of something in the plot, through the fish that turn in concentric circles and the siren heard in the distance. But to conclude from these examples that the characters are not thereby informed would be to miss an essential point. Claude's thoughts take the form of a question and of an "uneasy affirmation"; Kyo and Katow have just heard confirmed a report they had been expecting to hear all along. In both cases the dramatic intrusion informs the reader symbolically of what the characters already sense: the inexorable movement of destiny has begun. And in this sense they may be thought of as a kind of indirect discourse, the objectification of an inner, anxious awareness which works in such a way as to convey this same awareness to the mind of the reader so that he too must undergo a sense of anxiety.

In these and similar cases the message of the forewarning is eventually assimilated directly into the consciousness of the character, to be, once again, expressed through an image. An unusually dramatic instance occurs in the course of Tchen's espousal of his own ideology of terrorism and in its consummation. Just as he is about to reveal to his friends that the only efficient way to execute Chiang Kai-shek is through suicide, our eyes are directed upwards—and our minds towards a fatal plan: "The low, heavy clouds advanced in the same direction as they, beneath the yellowish daylight, with the unsettled but pressing movement of destinies." After he informs them of his plan (and before they accept it) they enter the back room of a shop, where the light marks a moment of suspense for us: "The back of the shop was lit only by the daylight reaching through the store. Because the sky was gray, a leaden light like the sort that precedes storms dominated the scene; in this dingy fog, light effects on the bellies of the hurricane lamps showed up as upside-down, parallel question marks." As Tchen continues to insist on their collaboration, he suddenly discovers what it is he really wants—and the darkness of fate moves in. "The reflections disappeared from the lamps. The light in the windowless room diminished: the clouds outside were probably thickening" (CH, pp. 314-15). The "probably" here is worthy of note. It would seem to reveal a narrating voice determined to squeeze every drop out of Tchen's experience, without, however, breaking the rules of perspective. The drama of destiny requires that the decor darken, but since we cannot see outside Malraux cannot report unequivocally that there are clouds there. But the "probably" also suggest that Tchen is aware of the darkness, so that once again we find an intrusive decor representing symbolically and dramatically an awareness in the character of a still undefined fate. Finally, the image which expresses destiny just as Tchen is about to throw himself upon his bomb— in this case, a flowing river—is not intruded by the narrator, but becomes part of Tchen's own consciousness: "Tchen watched all these shadows flowing in silence towards the river, inexplicably and unceasingly; was this force not Destiny itself which was prodding them towards the end of the avenue, where an archway lit by dim store signs just ahead of the darkness of the river seemed like the very doors of death?" (CH, p. 353).

Intrusions that serve as forewarnings seemingly to reader alone are relatively infrequent. More generally what the reader perceives is an exact report of what the character perceives. Malraux endows all his major characters, and many of the minor ones as well, with a remarkably well developed sensing apparatus, thus providing a considerable range of experienced phenomena for the narrating voice to focus the reader's attention upon—phenomena which are both external and internal to the characters. Further, from the examples above it should be clear that Malraux's narrating voice is itself a hypersensitive focusing mechanism which generally expects the reader's senses to perform the same sort of adjustments as those of the characters (in two of the novels, of course, character and narrating voice coincide: *Les Conquérants* and *Les Noyers de L'Altenburg*).

Notes

1. For a particularly well-developed discussion of this notion, see Eugene H. Falk, *Types of Thematic Structure* (Chicago: University of Chicago Press, 1967).

2. W. M. Frohock, ed., *Image and Theme: Studies in Modern French Fiction* (Cambridge, Mass.: Harvard University Press, 1969), p. 3.

3. Readers familiar with the work of Leo Spitzer will no doubt recognize here the principle of the "philological circle." I have not, however, consciously modeled my study on Spitzer's method.

4. Stephen Ullmann, *Style in the French Novel* (Cambridge: At the University Press, 1957), p. 213.

5. There are a total number of about 1,533 pages of text in the editions employed for this study, and a total number of about 3,200 analogical units counted, for an average of slightly more than two images per page of text. *Les Conquérants* gives the lowest average (1.7 images per page), *L'Espoir* the highest (2.5).

[2]

Imagery of Nature

The characters of Malraux's novels, as we have seen, are endowed with a remarkable capacity for sensing the elements that compose the universe. Behind the physio-neurological reactions of these characters we can readily perceive an author who is patently fascinated with the possibilities of creating complex perspectives, and who has developed a considerable facility in handling sensuous decor. Decor is considerably more than mere local color in Malraux's novels. The elements of nature—atmospheric presences, celestial bodies, water, earth, vegetation—are not there as ornaments, but to be sensed, to undergo subjective interpretation, and, through imagery, to become correlatives of private and universal experience.

The Sky, the Sun, Light

In his speech at the Altenburg, Möllberg uses an analogy to express a fundamental attitude of pessimism: "A sky is always a sky, whether it is gray, empty, or streaked with clouds; but the only common feature in these three cases is something through which it does not exist" (NA, p. 141). What Möllberg is challenging is the idea that history gives meaning to the human adventure; but let us consider for the moment not the idea expressed but the use of the analogy itself, and what it suggests about Malraux's treatment of decor as a figurative device. Whether the sky is filled with stars or clouds, for example, is quite irrelevant to any aspect of a novel's development until our attention is focused upon them, whereupon these exterior presences highlight a character's awareness of an object or event, and occasionally become an integral part of understanding itself.

A blank sky has no meaning in itself, but as the final possible resting place for the moving eye it often serves Malraux's purpose for setting up dramatic backdrops and for creating painterly effects. When the narrator of *Les Conquérants* makes his first penetration into a milling Asiatic city, he sees multicolored Chinese characters: "painted on vertical boards or fixed at eye-level or hanging high, on the rectangle of the sky, they surround me like a swarm of insects" (LC, p. 31). The sense of desolation is heightened in *L'Espoir* when what the eye perceives becomes a "cutout" upon the background of the sky: "at the end of the narrow streets, also fully lit up, illuminated better for death now than it had been earlier for tourists, strangely flat against the backdrop of the night sky, the Alcazar was in smoke" (LE, p. 592; see also LC, p. 38, VR, pp. 163, 237, 252, LE, p. 729, NA, p. 184).

The recurrent play of light and shadow in Malraux is a similar technique of dramatic highlighting, perhaps more reminiscent of the cinema than of painting.[1] We are introduced to the principal characters in *La Condition humaine,* for example, as a light swings back and forth over them, momentarily revealing each face in the shadows. The technique works quite well: the first time we see Kyo, we are immediately given an insight into a condition of alienation that will plague him throughout the novel:

> To the right, Kyo Gisors; swinging over his head, the lamp sharply accentuated the drooping corners of his mouth that seemed to belong to a Japanese print; swinging away it shifted the shadows and his half-breed face seemed almost European. The oscillations of the

> lamp became progressively shorter: Kyo's two faces were revealed, one after the other, less and less different from each other. (CH, p. 187)

Malraux casts rays of light onto objects like spotlights. A thick sunbeam bursts upon a long-coveted sculpture, for example, and Claude Vannec is filled with the sudden, dazzling joy of discovery (VR, p. 113). Even objects of peripheral interest seem to take on dramatic significance when they reflect light: a weapon lying near the corpse of a soldier (LC, p. 140), drops of blood glistening in the sun (VR, p. 214, LE, p. 478, LE, p. 571), a hammer momentarily useless against the hard stone of a sculpture (VR, p. 121). It is worth noting that an overall pattern of meaning is detectable here: what is often being focused upon is the cost of violent action, and perhaps, from a much broader perspective, the vanity of such action.

It is thus possible to discover in Malraux's use of the sky, the sun and light in general patterns of assigned meanings that go beyond dramatic technique. Daylight, for example, although providing no real analogies, frequently turns up in contexts which link it to notions of security and rationality. One of these is the instinctive feeling that men have that there is safety in the daytime, and a release from the anxieties of night. Before his last battle, Katow reflects: "It seemed that the fighting was slacking off along with night—and, absurdly, that this dawning day which showed not a single enemy shadow was bringing them freedom just as the night had brought them imprisonment" (CH, p. 381; see also VR, p. 183). Since day is the time of reason, it is opposed to killing. Klein tells the narrator of *Les Conquérants* that it is impossible to commit suicide during daylight (LC, p. 119). The narrator of *Les Noyers de l'Altenburg* feels that a shell aimed at his tank will not hit its target because killing takes place "only at night" (NA, p. 276).

Such associations are, of course, nothing more than animistic projections. The sky and light are eternal, phenomenological presences, in reality totally indifferent to man's fate; yet they can reflect man's bipolar sense of destiny. Light means life because it releases man from the intimacy of night and the self, and allows him to act upon the world. But light may become too strong, a crushing force that can obliterate man; hence its presence more often is associated with anxiety.

Malraux here seems to have applied to the condition of modern man the traditional lesson of Greek tragedy: to see light is to know, and it is good that man should want to know; but he may be punished for going too far. Gisors, perhaps the most fatalistic of Malraux's intellectuals, believes that "everyone suffers because everyone thinks" (CH, p. 430). Thus, in the closing pages of *La Condition humaine*, "contemplating the agitation of all these unknown beings who were walking towards death in the dazzling sunlight" (CH 430), the expression of Gisors's anxiety is related to the shining sun—an anxiety which he can relieve only through his opium pipe. In *Les Conquérants,* as anxiety mounts after the alleged suicide of Tcheng-Dai, the narrator reflects that the idea of *death* is as present as light (LC, p. 127). And in *Les Noyers de l'Altenburg,* Vincent Berger, profoundly disturbed by Möllberg's attack on the notion that the human adventure has meaning, goes out alone to watch the setting sun light up the orchards: "orchards of inexhaustible rebirths, forever lit up by the same anguish as by the same sun!" (NA, p. 151).

We may be dealing with more than decor, then, when we read that a character's eyes are dazzled by light. While it is not possible to establish an exact equivalence, on the whole the light might be read as an indication that forces stronger than the heroes are working to frustrate their activities—in short, as the presence of fate (see, for example, LC, pp. 59, 123, TM, p. 72, LE, p. 516).

During Perken's death scene, in the final section of *La Voie Royale,* the sun and light take on an increasingly explicit symbolic equivalence for man's paradoxical fate. Claude props up Perken's head: "Perken opened his eyes; he was invaded by the sky, crushing and yet full of joy" (VR, p. 263). He forgets everything else, and concentrates on the dazzling light: "he recognized nothing now beyond this immense expanse, white with light, this tragic joy into which he was fading" (VR, p. 264). The positive content of light, its element of "joy" for Perken, lies in the fact that "life was there, in the dazzling brightness into which the earth was fading" (VR, p. 264); the negative content is that its "implacable call" is the call to death. Perken's tragedy is that there cannot be one without the other: he clenches his teeth, "drunk with the desire to flee his body, with the desire not to give up this incandescent sky which was taking him like an animal" (VR, pp. 265-66). Finally, as he goes under, Claude watches him, reflecting: "anguish seemed unchanging like the sky above the funereal lamentation of the dogs" (VR, p. 267).

Why does Malraux have Perken, and no other of his heroes, undergo this particular way of dying in broad, dazzling daylight? A likely explanation is that in no other novel has Malraux created characters so openly defiant of fate. Grabot, in a large sense Perken's model for heroic action, had openly taunted fate by blinding himself in one eye, thereby proving that he was above accepting orders from men. Fate responded by blinding him in the other eye as well, and by transforming him from the overly proud victor into a slave for savage tribesmen. Perken hangs on to light and the sky during his last moments as to an opponent, because he, unlike Grabot, intends to win, and not be subdued by fate. He will, of course, die; but in his last words, "There is no . . . no death . . . There is only . . . *me* . . . *me* about to die . . .," he asserts the inviolability of the self. Unlike Grabot, he will remain lucid unto the very moment of death, fully and proudly in possession of himself. In the total context of all Malraux's work one might judge Perken's defiance of fate as an unsatisfactory, egocentric gesture, but in the context of the novel itself, it is clear that Malraux means for Perken's death to take on the grandeur of a tragic model.

In *L'Espoir* we find a character who cannot get enough light. Jaime, blinded during an airplane battle, longs to see again, and at one point actually begins to think he can see lights. The scene in question is a subtly constructed passage of ironic juxtaposition. Jaime's remarks are interspersed periodically throughout a wide-ranging conversation that his comrades in the airbrigade are having: " 'I see lights,' said Jaime . . . . 'The lights are turning,' said Jaime, who had removed his black glasses. . . . 'The lights are stopping,' said Jaime. . . . 'Do you see the lights?' asked Jaime." (LE, pp. 788, 789, 790) Towards the end of the recorded conversation, Malraux writes of Scali, one of several characters in the book who try to make sense of the bewildering variety of attitudes held by fighting men:

> For twenty years Scali had heard people speak of the "notion of man." And he had beat his head against the wall thinking about it. It was just so much talk, this notion of man, given the reality of man acting out life and death! Scali clearly no longer knew what was what. (LE, p. 790).

The sense of this episode must clearly be sought through the orchestration of its elements. The main context consists of men at war expressing desires and attitudes that are somehow incongruous given the historical import of the present moment. There is a blind man who provides a chorus when he says he thinks he sees lights, and then loses them—symbolically, the lights must be interpreted as understanding. And there is the intellectual, the man for whom Malraux has set up the symbol, who is constantly baffled in his attempt to create a unified image of Man on the basis of the men around him.

Night, Darkness, Shadows

Malraux's characters often seem to be united by the force of night. The effect can be considered positive, however, only in that fraternal union is strong enough to transcend darkness. Night dramatizes union and tends to render it tragic, as in this example: "At the same time that nocturnal friendship was bringing him closer to Tchen, a strong sense of helplessness penetrated Kyo, the anxiety of being only a man, only himself" (CH, p. 287). Under most conditions, night and darkness are a force, frequently personified, or a region, relating to negative states of the soul.

The image appears with particular frequency in three of the novels. In *La Voie Royale* night is linked to the primordial nature of the jungle and its savages, so that the heroes' adventure takes on the format of a journey into the "heart of darkness" (for examples see VR, pp. 38, 161, 98, 202, 208). In *La Condition humaine* Malraux has created a truly "dark" hero: Tchen. He murders his first victim in a darkened room at night; and even as he does so, his "interior" darkness is expressed as being deeper than the exterior one: "beneath his sacrifice to the revolution swarmed a world of depths compared to which this night crushed with anxiety was all brightness" (CH, pp. 181-82). The night motif underscores in Tchen a depth of solitude, an imprisonment within the primordial self, probably unmatched by any other of Malraux's characters. As a terrorist, he has become an agent of fatality, himself an active force of darkness: "But it was far off that men dwelled; here nothing remained of the world other than a night to which Tchen was instinctively attuned as though to a new friendship: this nocturnal, disquieting world was not opposed to murder" (CH, p. 187). He will die at night in his final attempt to assassinate Chiang Kai-shek, after his attempt, which had taken place in the early afternoon, had resulted in failure.

In *Le Temps du mépris* night and darkness become appropriate images for conveying aspects of Kassner's anguished imprisonment. His hopelessness is expressed as "dark shadows" (TM, p. 102); darkness and night bind him (TM, p. 48), and deprive him of his will: "He was an animal of action, and the dark shadows were releasing him from the intoxication of his will" (TM, p. 46). When he recalls the real night, outside, it is in terms of the tragedy-tinged fraternal union noted above: "night was falling over the entire universe, a night in which men know each other walking together or in silence, abandoned night, full of stars and friendship" (TM, p. 59). But even this is soon transformed, under the weight of his own despair, and he feels there is nothing around him but stone and "the other night, dead night" (TM, p. 60).

Malraux's heroes must grapple with an enormous mass of literal and figurative darkness in the course of their confrontations with hard reality. It is not surprising, then, that the novels are permeated with those areas situated between darkness and light: shadows. At the literal level, Malraux's shadows may obscure or confuse vision, contrast with light to create theatrical effects, or hint at some sinister, even tragic presence. The figurative shadows perform a variety of functions, expressing such qualities as faintness or pervasiveness (see, for example, VR, p. 197, CH, p. 181, CH, p. 184), or else the whole universe of nameless men, such as in this instance: "those who made three hundred million miserable men aware of their revolt were not shadows like men who pass by" (CH, p. 428; see also CH, p. 371, NA, p. 27).

But by far the greater number of shadow images appear as simple synecdoches. Rather than name the designated object, Malraux will frequently choose to present its dark aura as the being itself. The shadow may apply to a named character; significantly, it appears several times in the case of Tchen alone. In order to see his first victim closely, for example, Tchen must enter the light and let his "squat shadow" pass over the bed (CH, p. 182). Or when he explains his terrorist creed to his two accomplices, we read: "Tchen's shadow, too vague to be a silhouette, advanced over the worried eyes of the others" (CH, p. 315). The shadow quite frequently refers to masses of people or to anonymous individuals, particularly in *La Condition humaine*, *L'Espoir* and *Les Noyers de l'Altenburg,* novels in which much of the action takes place against a backdrop of the faceless poor, workers, soldiers, etc. Some examples: "But the voices became silent and low shadows, on the sidewalk, revealed that three bodies were there. The police?" (CH, p. 310); "Upon the walls and shop window shutters shadows moved, leaning forward, parallel like boat haulers" (LE, p. 690); "Each morning I look at thousands of shadows in the unsteady light of dawn, and I think: 'This is man' " (NA, p. 27). Finally, Malraux's fascination with the shadow can be further appreciated when we consider that he uses it to apply to parts of the human body, to inanimate objects, animals, and even abstractions: "The shadow of his solid nose, projected on the whitewashed wall, chipped off a corner of a Cambodian painting" (VR, p. 72); "the car came grinding out of the large oblique shadow of the building" (LC, p. 85); "the shadow of a butterfly danced upon his face" (LE, p. 488); "a shadow of passion slipped into Vologuine's voice" (CH, p. 286), etc.

Stars

There is little reason to distinguish between Malraux's use of *étoile, astre* or *constellation*; no matter how expressed, their analogical content, from the first to the last novel, is consistently and manifestly that of fate. For a character such as Hemmelrich, almost physically frustrated from being a free man, the stars suggest suffering: "there was more pain in the world than stars in the sky" (CH, p. 312). An intellectual such as Kassner will see in the stars a universal condition in which man is blindly subservient to death: "this casually demented crowd which did not perceive in itself that thing that corresponded to lurking death, up there, in its steppes of stars" (TM, p. 153).

If there is any greatness in man, then, it may lie in his capacity to overturn the logic of the stars. This is what Walter Berger experiences after listening to Nietzsche's voice: "Sometimes . . . the thousands of stars in the sky seemed to me as diminished by man as our paltry destinies are diminished by the starry sky" (NA, p. 97). But the narrator of the novel goes on to make an anguishing distinction, one which appears as a theme in the latter three novels: "This privilege of which Walter spoke—how much more powerful it was against the starry sky than against pain!" (NA, p. 99). Art can be used as a weapon against the stars—that is, it can achieve for man a kind of victory over death—but it can never efface suffering while man is still living.

A contemplation of the stars thus evokes a reaction of anxiety in Malraux's characters or conveys anxiety directly to the reader. After his first murder, Tchen steps out onto the balcony of his victim's room, high above the streets of Shanghai, and we read: "In the rip made by the clouds, stars settled into their eternal movement which invaded him along with the cooler air outside" (CH, p. 184). At this moment Tchen is in full harmony with his fate, which is to be separated definitively from the world of men (that is, men who do not murder). Once he is down on the street, something makes him look up at the sky: "Without knowing why, Tchen looked at it: how much closer he had been to it, a while before, when he had discovered the stars! He left it progressively further behind him as his anxiety diminished, as he rediscovered men" (CH, p. 186).

In *Le Temps du mépris,* the star images coincide for the most part with the section in which night images abound: the early part of Kassner's imprisonment, during which he is most helpless to combat his overwhelming sense of anxiety. Here we read that his hallucinatory visions gravitate "with the imperceptible movement of constellations" (TM, p. 54). His body becomes confused with the unending "fate of stars" (TM, p. 56). He has intimations of a fate (to be understood here in its clearest sense as a determinism oblivious to man's will to act) as a *double* imprisonment: "the stars would always pass over the same places of this sky constellated with fate, and forever would these imprisoned stars turn within this imprisoned immensity, like the men imprisoned in this jail and him in his cell" (TM, p. 60).

Walter Berger speaks of the feeling of anxiety as a vertigo, in the heavily Pascalian section of *Les Noyers de l'Altenburg* in which the star motif abounds: "But I know that certain works resist the vertigo born when we meditate upon our dead ones, upon the starry sky, upon history" (NA, p. 98). The contexts in which the star motif is found permit several themes to be associated within a single complex of anxiety-provoking realities: silence, solitude, imprisonment, and death (see, for example, LC, p. 38, VR, pp. 156, 161, CH, p. 186, TM, pp. 53, 59, 75, LE, p. 627, NA, p. 99). Even where inclusion of stars into innumerable settings, then, seems no more than a dramatic visual effect, their mere presence can induce the sensation of a sobering awareness. The same can probably be said of Malraux's references to "stars" which are not heavenly bodies at all: stars doodled on a tablecloth, decorating a church dome, reflected in windows, or strewn as flowers along a battlefield (TM, p. 59, LE, p. 741, NA, pp. 150, 179).

There is much to suggest, in all these contexts, a richly elaborated scenario on Malraux's part. When the stars are visible, or spoken of, or artificially evoked, there occurs a kind of introspection into man's condition which is associated with feelings of anxiety and, quite often as well, with a sense of paralysis: the stars show men the limits of their freedom. But a sky in which the stars are rendered invisible by fog, clouds, or smoke allows for a considerable amount of action—action which can be viewed essentially as a revolt against man's fate.

Atmospheric Presences: Clouds, Fog, Mist, Smoke

Malraux is particularly fond of depicting clouds that hover over scenes of activity, reflecting against the higher backdrop of the sky the undertakings of men on earth. In *La Voie Royale* Claude wonders whether or not his party can ever penetrate the heavy jungle to discover the lost sculptures he is seeking, and decides that if others have done so, he can too; but we are immediately forewarned: "Against this uneasy affirmation, the overcast sky and the inextricable matting of insect-studded leaves opposed their silent affirmation" (VR, p. 57). In *Le Temps du mépris* Malraux personifies the clouds as the enemy, with its own laws, as Kassner's plane struggles against a great storm as in some great primitive combat. Kassner discovers his own minuscule size in contrast to an enormous black cloud, no longer calm and motionless above, but ready to spring, "alive and murderous," having its own laws and the primitive voice of an old, powerful enemy (TM, pp. 133-35). Clouds, then, may become a challenge that invites the man of strong will to combat; Vincent Berger states as much himself: a man who is free to choose the country he will serve will look for the country that offers "the biggest clouds" (NA, p. 66).

Early in *La Condition humaine* Malraux assigns the clouds the role which they are to play in that novel:

> The low and heavily massed clouds, torn in places, no longer allowed the last stars to be seen in the depths of their rips. This life of the clouds—sometimes lighter, sometimes heavier—animated the darkness as if enormous shadows had come to deepen night. (CH, p. 192)

A significant pattern develops: the clouds in such scenes, by masking the stars which symbolize fatality, allow men to perform their duties beyond a conscious awareness of their fatality. Equally significant is the implicit link that has been established between clouds and men themselves, since the clouds are made participants in the action. Just as Tchen is about to reveal to his two accomplices that the only way to consummate the assassination of Chiang Kai-shek is through suicide, our eyes are directed upwards to low clouds advancing along with the three men: "The low and heavy clouds advanced in the direction in which they were walking, below the yellowish sky, with a movement which was unsettled yet pressing with destinies" (CH, p. 314). Similarly, clouds seem to follow the movement of combat planes, a battle column, lines of soldiers, and fires (LE, pp. 555, 755, 843, NA, p. 234). Such images underscore, dramatically, the direction of human destiny: men act, and the universe at the same time gives meaning to their acts and an epic grandeur to those engaged in the struggle.

But just as literal clouds are ephemeral, so too are men and their endeavors; and the image of a sky which absorbs clouds comes to represent human transiency. Perken, just before he dies, reflects: "no man had ever died, ever: they had passed on like the clouds which just a short while before had become absorbed into the sky, like the forest, like the temples; only he was going to die, be snatched away" (VR, p. 265). The image expresses succinctly the difference between the notion that an egocentric man is likely to have of other men's dying—a notion conceived in the serene certitude of life—and the brutal revelation of his own imminent death. Kyo compares the ephemeral happiness of his love for May to a cloud "which is absorbed into the gray sky" (CH, p. 214). And Gisors, unlike Perken in his capacity for serene, poignant contemplation, stifles his sorrow over the death of Kyo, and discovers in the thinning clouds the men he has lost forever:

> Light, and very high up, the clouds passed over the dark pines and were absorbed bit by bit into the sky; and he thought that one of their groups—that one, exactly—expressed the men he had known or loved, and who had died. (CH, p. 431)

The function of Malraux's fog and mist images stems naturally from their properties of density. They cast a heavy veil over the action, concealing and distorting shapes, and are an appropriate figure for indicating what is unseen, unknown, hence insecure. As Kyo watches May suffer, her face seems to have sunk into a fog (CH, p. 214); Gisors, seeking help for Kyo, must rely upon Clappique's "hands of fog" (CH, p. 375; see also VR, p. 209, CH, p. 385).

When destiny imposes its order over human will, Malraux may express it in terms of a fog which obliterates straight lines. Just before Tchen's attempted assassination of Chiang Kai-shek, the fog "destroys" the sidewalks (CH, p. 353). Kassner, returning home from prison, perceives that the lines in the palm of his hand and the lines of the earth are equally "consumed" by fog and night (TM, p. 145). It should be apparent, then, why so much literal fog is present just before, and during, certain kinds of scenes: Malraux is highlighting a zone of imminent—and extremely dramatic—danger. Tchen, hoping to kill Chiang Kai-shek, waits in "cities of mist" (CH, p. 352); as Clappique gambles away the whole revolutionary cause at a nightclub, tobacco smoke is described as a "fog" (CH, p. 357); Kassner's plane must pass through a "realm of fog" before reaching safety (TM, p. 132), etc. In *Les Noyers de l'Altenburg*, there are two such danger zones. A mass of poison gas advances fatally in the form of a yellow fog (NA, p. 203) until it reaches its destination, the Russian lines, where it becomes literally poison gas. Similarly, as a tank turns off the road to cross a field enshrouded in fog, the men within know they have entered an insecure world; in fact, they will fall into a tank trap (NA, p. 266-68). And yet the presence of fog may also indicate favorable human activity in spite of the forces of destiny. As the people of Madrid in *L'Espoir* hurry to set up a street barricade for defense against the Franco army, a thick fog settles over them: "in all the streets that radiated about the square, the same shadows, as faithful as the fog, were working at the same barricades" (LE, p. 694).

Malraux introduces into his novels numerous other atmospheric motifs in addition to the clouds and fog considered above. Some are little more than clichés: distant military noises sound like thunder and hail (LC, p. 93, CH, p. 244, LE, p. 747); heat transforms a city into an oven (LC, p. 30), etc. The more interesting ones are those in which literal presences are elaborated in some way, either heightening sensous effects or bringing personified forces into play.

The wind and air, for example, are frequently introduced to carry noises and odors, and to bring movement into a still decor. The effect is dramatic rather than sensuous, however. Malraux employs it most often at the end of narrative segments, rather like the fade-out technique of the cinema:

> A very light wind from the bay softly lifts the mats stretched across the windows, revealing a triangle of white wall covered with sleeping lizards, and carries the smell of hot tar from the road; occasionally, only the sound of a distant siren, alone and as though smothered, comes up from the sea . . . .(LC, p. 36)

In *La Condition humaine*, a sky filled with smoke seems to participate in men's activities exactly as do the cloud images:

> Over the cruisers and ships which could not unload their cargoes arose slanting masses of smoke which the heavy wind blew in the direction that the rebels were taking, as though the sky were participating in the rebellion. (CH, p. 246)

In *La Voie Royale* various atmospheric images create a claustrophobic setting in which Perken's death will be played out. Columns of smoke rising over the native fires strewn over the jungle seem to drive Perken inexorably toward his retreat, and take on the symbolic proportions of prison bars as he is slowly overcome by the jungle heat: "more and more numerous, enormous and vertical in the noonday furnace, the smoke from the Meis' fires was blocking the horizon like gigantic bars" (VR, pp. 261-62; and see VR, pp. 238, 239, 240, 242); death surrounds him as far as the horizon "like the trembling air" (VR, p. 265); and his final memories become "as thick as this smoke" (VR, p. 265).

In *L'Espoir*, a number of episodes are played out against the backdrop of blazing buildings and cities. These are no doubt representations of real historical events that took place during the Spanish Civil War—but they also furnish Malraux the material for considerable imaginative elaboration. Fires ravaging a church in Toledo, for example, eat away at the statues of saints creating a new artistic style:

> Manuel watched in admiration, and again felt like an artist: these contorted statues were finding in the extinguished fire a barbaric grandeur, as though their dance had been born here of the flames, as though this style had suddenly become that of the fire itself. (LE, p. 580)

Fire thus becomes associated with the theme of the Apocalypse in *L'Espoir*; soldiers stir like flames, smoke makes war and advances, while the holocaust of Madrid becomes a world of fire, a new "Age of Fire" (LE, pp. 622, 634, 757).

Vegetation and Earth

The world of vegetation provides Malraux a wide source of picturesque detail with which to paint decors and establish correspondences. It is not unusual to find here analogies which are stretched quite far. Fairly typical is an image in which the length of night is compared to the length of leaves in the surrounding jungle: "this world in which the nights lengthened like the leaves" (VR, p. 235). The abstractness here of temporal duration is given the concreteness of spatial length through little more than a similarity of vocabulary and, of course, the author's patent interest in making sensuous connections at a number of levels. In another instance, the raised hands of soldiers stir like nearby leaves floating in the air (LE, p. 794); the analogy thus tends to set up a visual prolongation of a movement, amplifying it and imparting a set, painterly quality to it.

Malraux often employs images of fruits and vegetables to create simple visual effects. When applied to persons they are little more than comic clichés: a head is bean-shaped (CH, p. 399), a nose is like a beet (NA, p. 258), a face like a string bean (LE, p. 583); a small man resembles black olives (LE, p. 652), a fat one an apple (LE, p. 798). Applied to groups of people the cliché is likely to depict misery: the poor have pear-shaped bellies (LC, p. 56) and mandragora limbs (LC, p. 144). Applied to objects the image may again be a cliché: an artichoke illustrates the shape of flames (LE, p. 721), a foggy light is expressed as moss (LC, p. 56), and a plane dive as a vine tendril (LE, p. 664). But frequently in *L'Espoir* the images take on the surprise effect of a genuine poetic figure, sustaining the impression that in this novel more than any other Malraux is intent upon achieving striking visual effects: a Spanish hotel tower resembles a pineapple (LE, p. 451), Toledo under cloudy skies takes on the tones of black grapes (LE, p. 622) while night takes on the color of eggplant (LE, p. 623). The latter images suggest that Malraux might well have visualized Toledo through the perspective of an El Greco painting.

Simple mineral images refer almost exclusively to color: salt expresses brilliant whiteness (VR, p. 124), copper applies to the sun (NA, p. 142), and the image of chalk conveys a dusty color (LC, p. 112, VR, pp. 252-53, LE, p. 580). Lead appears with the greatest frequency, painting elements in the landscape; they are related to Malraux's use of low clouds to create brooding atmospheres as well as to his penchant for using painterly techniques for dramatic highlighting (CH, pp. 314-15, TM, p. 134, LE, p. 669, NA, p. 225).

The narrator of *Les Conquérants* describes Hong Kong, seen from a distance, as follows: "it is not a silhouette, a paper cutout surface, but something solid and deep like real matter, like a black earth" (LC, p. 29). From his first novel on there is a recurrent tendency in Malraux's use of decor to show distinctions between flat perspectives and three-dimensional ones, expressing that which in the universe is ephemeral in contrast to what is solid, profound, and very likely eternal. Solidity and profundity take on several figurative forms: heavy weights, stonelike hardness, petrification, and the permanent immobility of objects. These communicate a sense of a universe hostile to man—hostile because they represent an obtuseness in the reality against which men throw themselves in their attempts to change the order of things, and also because they are the eternal reminder of man's own transiency as opposed to that of the world.

One of the more interesting patterns in this group has to do with being underground. Malraux writes of Gisors, reflecting just before taking a dose of opium: "This strength, this raging underground imagination which was in himself (if I were to go mad, he had thought, this alone would remain of me) was ready to take on all forms" (CH, p. 229). The underground image here expresses the critical distinction, explored throughout this novel, between what is exterior to the self—hence active, and capable of union with others—and that which is most private to the self: an imagination which does not realize itself in the world, a solitary imprisonment, an essential madness. Kassner, in prison, places his faith in "that underground area where music takes a man's head between her hands to raise it slowly towards manly brotherhood" (TM, p. 57) until he realizes the need to conquer "his dazed state, and madness, and the obsession of escaping that continued its underground life" (TM, p. 68) and to organize his thoughts in the real world. Perken, in *La Voie Royale*, imagines death as an underground place: "A gallery was waiting for him, about to cave in, buried deep under the earth" (VR, p.266). The image informs us of what death means for him: a definitive loss of the exterior world of action. These images underscore Malraux's tendency to situate some of his episodes in literal underground areas to create predicaments which embody descents into hell. Kyo's and Kassner's stay in prison, Attignies's voyage through a tunnel in *L'Espoir* and the narrator's fall into a tank pit in *Les Noyers de l'Altenburg* provide some of the more eloquent examples in the novels.

Just as Malraux's earth and stone imagery connotes permanence, so dust, flying leaves, and decomposition express impermanence; these three groups of images appear with very great frequency in the novels. As an equivalent for human weakness, the dust and flying leaf images express the absence of an effective contact with reality, hence a feeling of futility or absurdity. Towards the end of *Le Temps du mépris* Kassner tells his wife: 'Joy is always a bit like that—whirling leaves . . . fluttering on the surface" (TM, p. 175). In taking on his high adventure, Claude Vannec wishes to escape man's usual fate of a "life of dust" (VR, pp. 55-56). And Vincent Berger, visiting one desert tribe after the other to stir up enthusiasm for political unity, soon discovers the futility of dealing with tribes on the verge of "falling into dust" (NA, p. 70). Clearly we are dealing here with one of Malraux's most persistent themes, man's need to grasp life concretely and to transcend in some manner his sense of insecurity brought on by his mortal condition.

The presence of this kind of imagery is particularly prevalent in four of the novels. In *La Voie Royale* Malraux exploits every facet of jungle vegetation to plunge his heroes into a state of primitivism, applying a number of plant analogies to evoke impressions of imprisonment and madness (see, for example, VR, pp. 97, 149, 192, 195, 232, 265). There are, in effect, two separate journeys into this "heart of darkness," in each of which there is an object, a central focus, informing us of the sense of the adventure. In the first it is a stone sculpture, primarily the goal of Claude's quest. What ideally represented for him a valuable artifact of human art and culture (and, of course, potential financial profit) is revealed as an enormously hostile block of matter which must be wrested by brute force from the immobile universe which had claimed it over the centuries. There is a victory of sorts over the stone, but the almost indifferent treatment Malraux accords this victory, as well as the subsequent development in plot, implies that the victory is a Pyrrhic one. The effect is that Claude has finally discovered the eventual limits to his own human force in the face of the power of the objective world.

In the second of the adventures, the central object is the discovery of Grabot, the "great white hunter" who has now become the miserable slave of savage tribesmen. Finding him is primarily the goal of Perken's quest, and whereas in the first adventure we found a concrete reminder of a hostile universe, here we focus upon a forceful Western man who has become a testimonial to the illusion of human force. When Claude and Perken enter Grabot's hut, light penetrates "like a block of stone"; he is attached to a stone mill; and when we have a closer look at him we see the colorless skin of a man who has lived in a cellar, with a wrestler's shoulders: "a powerful ruin." Meanwhile, the novel has been served by no fewer than fifteen images having to do with crushing, depicting the malevolent forces of sun, jungle and time that work against the heroes and embodying the vanity of their venture; and no fewer than nineteen images of decomposition relating to the characters. Early on in the novel Claude announces to a government official that his reason for being in Asia is to study art: "You might say that in art, time does not exist. What interests me, you see, is decomposition—the transformation of these works, the deepest aspects of their lives, which is made out of the death of men" (VR, p. 61). His interest will be more than gratified; he will enter a literally rotting world with Perken, who thinks of himself and his own projects in terms of rot (VR, pp. 88, 90, 259, 261), will himself undergo a decomposition of mind (VR, pp. 97, 124) and finally discover this Western man, Grabot, in as sure a state of disintegration (VR, pp. 185, 192) as the Oriental savages, who might well have deteriorated from a higher culture capable of producing the temple art Claude wishes to secure.

In *Le Temps du mépris* images of crushing weight and decomposition of mind and soul simply underscore what we are aware of in the literal context of Kassner's stone prison cell. Here again we are dealing with someone who must live like a man in a cellar—blind to the outside world, forced to live in a primitive state that brings him close to madness, and totally without power to pit himself against the hostile forces of the universe. If he is eventually released, it is not because of any act of his own—Kassner might well have become another Grabot—but because Malraux has by this time discovered a possibility for transcending the individual condition of men through the organized efforts of men united by political ideology.

In *L'Espoir* Malraux seems to have found an esthetic device for dealing with his newly optimistic position that men united can effectively shape human destiny, and that is a kind of epic style. His heroes are no longer locked in a steaming jungle, or paralyzed by glances towards the stars or a stone, or imprisoned within crushing cell walls. Armies now march or roll along the surface of an earth which has itself become the goal of heroic men. Images continue to evoke the pathos of dying men and the insufficiency of human force, but the perspective has now become more panoramic. Men disperse or lie dead, for example, like falling leaves (LE, pp. 654, 794); and the earth may become an indifferent scene upon which man's efforts are played out, as in this instance: "The approaching evening lent an infinite vanity to the eternal effort of men which the darkness and the indifference of the earth slowly enveloped" (LE, p. 578). But the earth can also become a personified force, participating jointly in the battle: "Through the furor with which the earth, which was exploding for kilometers around, seemed to rear up against the clouds, throw up against the winter rain its own gushing rain of clods, stones and wounds, Manuel saw an enemy wave arrive" (LE, p. 736). And throughout the novel the sounds of military activity, both friendly and hostile, are reverberated through an earth which the characters can feel physically and not merely imagine in their anxiety (see, for example, LE, pp. 654, 717, 720, 740). Towards the end of the novel, culminating the dramatic sequence during which wounded airmen are lovingly brought down from a mountainside by the population of an entire village, Magnin's eyes are directed towards a low apple tree growing along the route: "Its apples had not been picked—they had fallen, forming around it a thick ring which gradually thinned out into the grass. This apple tree was the only living thing in the stone, living the unceasingly renewed life of plants, in the geological indifference" (LE, p. 827). Here, finally, is a significant instance of a character who beholds a non-human, eternal force in Nature and relates it favorably to man. As he watches the line of men bringing down the wounded, against the backdrop of deeply cut mountain gorges, the apple tree—standing in its circle of dead, rotting and germinating fruit—seems to become, "beyond the life and death of men, the rhythm of the life and death of the earth." And he establishes the connection—not with the life of individual man, but with the race of man eternally renewed through time: "the solemn, primitive march of these stretchers, all this was as majestic as the pale rocks plunging downward from the heavy sky, as the eternity of apples scattered on the earth" (LE, p.835). The sense that seems to prevail over the final portion of this novel, and throughout the next, is the need to guarantee the rescue of Man.

Finally, *Les Noyers de l'Altenburg* is served by a particularly elaborate interplay of plant and earth imagery, sustaining the tone of reflection and of mysterious revelation that characterizes this book. As the novel opens the narrator states, without explanation, his fascination with something covering the cathedral floor, something "we thought we would never see again: straw" (NA, p. 13). In the course of the book there will be two descents into the world of death, each followed by a sense of the miraculous rebirth of life—not simply a sense of relief that the character has not died, but a joyous awareness of the tenacity of Life itself. In both instances, the presence of straw contributes to this feeling. Coming out of the area destroyed by poison gas, the narrator's father, Vincent, looks down at the ground to discover field grass, and insects made of "the same light straw"; and he reflects: "Just as the gas had mingled everything into a universal purulence, life seemed to be reborn from a single matter, from this straw" (NA, p. 242). At the end of the book, the narrator himself, saved from death in a tank pit, comes upon a barnyard strewn with straw, in which a simple straw broom suddenly becomes for him a flower born of humanity, bearing the mystery of life itself (NA, pp. 286-87). It is from the most ordinary, the most fundamental, that rays of hope emerge.

Vincent's adventures can be seen as a condensed recapitulation of the kinds of activities that Malraux's earlier heroes had engaged in. In going off to the Asiatic steppes to infuse political awareness into local tribesmen, he is reminiscent of a Garine, Perken or Grabot—a European manipulator of the masses in a foreign culture—though, unlike the earlier heroes, Vincent does not seem to be doing this out of an anxious need to cultivate his own sense of power. What he discovers in short order is an "ossified" society (NA, pp. 69, 72), requiring for renewal—if renewal were possible—a kind of conviction on Vincent's part which he simply does not have. Upon returning to Europe and the War, he is involved in the kind of intelligence work which calls for considerable compromise with his sense of integrity—somewhat reminiscent of certain situations in *L'Espoir*—and again he abandons the task (more will be said on this later). In joining an actual fighting group, involved in trench warfare, Vincent may be obeying an instinctive urge in certain of Malraux's heroes to associate with very ordinary men in group action at a critical moment, rather like the grand moments of virile fraternity that we see in *La Condition humaine* and *L'Espoir*. It is not unlikely that Malraux invented this segment in order for Vincent to perceive where his true conviction lay, and that is to rescue ordinary man from total oblivion. The episode in which poison gas will transform the forest and men—enemy men, at that—into rot, takes on the proportions of a metaphysical chaos unendurable to Malraux. The gas transforms vegetation into lichen, dead and rotting leaves, watercress (NA, pp. 218, 221, 225, 229), and the hair of poisoned soldiers turns into tobacco (NA, p. 224). The cliché of a cluster is reinforced for ironic effect as it depicts dead bees and dead men (NA, pp. 219, 232). The adjective 'petrified' is applied to a now dead tree and to the stiffness of dead soldiers in a trench (NA, pp. 219, 232).

Once the task of rescuing the poisoned men is accomplished, and he is out of the poisoned area, Vincent catches the smells of a fresh forest, and finds himself facing a copse of walnut trees—and he is suddenly reminded of the talks at the Altenburg and Möllberg's pessimistic conclusion that there is *no* unity to the human adventure. Profoundly disturbed at that time by the intellectual content of Möllberg's demonstrations, Vincent had none the less been unable to assimilate it to an intuitive feeling he had about the human adventure—and Malraux subtly underscores that intuition. The Altenburg dialogue itself is only the center of a much larger frame of phenomenal reality that captures Vincent's attention: the presence of walnut. Outside there are loggers piling up tree trunks exactly as medieval loggers piled up trunks, in the very same forest (NA, p. 141); inside, Möllberg's audience is in a priory decorated in medieval walnut. And when Vincent goes out of the Altenburg he beholds apple orchards "of inexhaustible rebirths" and thick old walnut trees "snatching the forces of the earth" to spread them out into branches "in an eternal life," imposing upon his mind "at the same time the idea of a will and of endless metamorphosis." Vincent's intuition now returns at the end of the Apocalypse of destruction represented by the poison gas episode to ponder the "mystery which would not yield its secret but only its presence" (NA, p. 244)—a mystery which at a universal level, as we have seen, has to do with the sheer tenacity of life itself, and at the human level with the idea of a will to continue—through eternal metamorphoses, perhaps, but still fundamentally as Man.

This mystery is recapitulated at the very end of the novel. The narrator, Vincent's son, and his group come across an old peasant couple, epitomized as a representation of the sheer human will to live, to age and to survive despite all of life's vicissitudes; the old woman, with a smile on her worn face, seems to be "leaning against the cosmos like a stone." We find among the great accumulation of analogies suggesting a miraculous revelation two elaborate images of germination. Night is no longer "the sepulchre of the pit" but a living night that seems "like a prodigious gift, like an immense germination" (NA, p. 284); the narrator bears within him "the irruption of earthly night," a "germination in the darkness" that virtually transforms the night into a womb which delivers over a new life to "the miraculous revelation of day" (NA, pp. 289-90).

Water and Sea Imagery

Malraux's water images—analogies to water movements, immersion in water, bodies of water—appear with considerable frequency. Flowing water—floods, drifting, agitated water movements, seething—these serve Malraux's need in all his novels to depict movement of many sorts. Crowd scenes—Asiatic in *Les Conquérants* and *La Condition humaine,* Spanish in *L'Espoir*—usually come across as massive and disorderly flows, as in this instance: "The car horn howled in vain, powerless against the force of this exodus, against this millenary seething that invasions stir up ahead of them" (CH, p. 241; see also LC, p. 58, CH, p. 353, LE, pp. 627, 691, 794, 795, 796, 797).

L'Espoir is particularly rich in images of water movements. Shells and exploding debris spurt like geysers: "Hit by the grenades, the tiles began to spurt up like a geyser" (LE, p. 571; see also LE, pp. 663, 712, 730, 768). They fall back to the earth like rain: "An explosion as if the earth had split somewhere in its depths brings a rainfall of leaves and twigs" (LE, p. 631, see also LE, pp. 458, 736). Smoke and fire flow and seethe, as in this instance where Manuel watches the smoke that follows an explosion in the Alcazar: "It advanced, not in jostled masses, but as water flows, piling up in holes and crevasses" (LE, p. 634; see also LE, pp. 721, 722, 791, 819). Such images endow war and its destruction with a universal pervasiveness, providing vivid physical correlatives for the abstract theme of the Apocalypse which dominates a good portion of the novel.

Images of immersion in water occur less frequently. The act of washing, or taking a bath, may express a feeling of release and relaxation. When Kassner's cell door is opened, light from the corridor "streamed down over his whole body, washed him of the darkness gluing his eyelids together" (TM, p. 112); in another image "fresh air relaxes us like a bath" (LC, p. 14). But other images of immersion evoke the

rising and falling alternatively to hide and then reveal the savage warriors facing him (VR, p. 210). Surf and tide imagery most frequently convey the overwhelming surge of fear and anxiety. Kassner believes mistakenly for a moment that the walls of his cell are coming in on him; "no, it was the tide of anxiety that surged with each droning throb of his temples" (TM, p. 77).

Images of a sea that strews debris along the shore appear in the last two novels, giving dramatic substance to panoramic scenes of desolation. In a couple of instances the debris relates to objects abandoned by fleeing masses: "The crowd, shaken on all sides, seethed about the first village, and left a thousand instruments about the first walls, as the sea at ebb tide leaves behind a shore of pebbles and debris" (LE, p. 797). In other instances the debris consists of dead soldiers; an assault wave, swept down by machine gun fire, "left its garland of dead, and ebbed back" (LE, p. 455). The element of poignancy in such images becomes more explicit when the debris consists of men run aground in the course of their heroic ventures. Kyo, about to be executed, thinks of Katow as a "condemned life, run aground against his own in the shadows full of threats and wounds" (CH, p. 403). Soldiers wounded in a noble cause, and now reduced to shadow, fill a hospital ward with "the brotherhood of the shipwrecked" (LE, p. 800; see also LC, p. 68, LE, p. 654, VR, p. 161).

Malraux's analogies to ships and boats, dock workers and boat haulers, give further evidence of his interest in activities related to the sea. These images appear in a variety of contexts. Some establish simple comparisons: animal horns are as wide across as boats (VR, p. 108); the sounds of sirens and horns are reminiscent of departing ships (LE, pp. 448, 449, 723), etc. The image of a wake provides visual depth to scenes of moving crowds and vehicles (LC, p. 146, LE, p. 633, NA, p. 203). It is worth noting that the more realistic, or colorful, of such images appear principally in the first two novels, perhaps the imaginative residue of Malraux's long sea voyages of the 1920s. The political talk overheard at a dinner by the narrator of *Les Conquérants* consists of "formulas, ludicrous in Europe, gathered here like old steamships covered with rust" (LC, p. 22). A Mei guide, taking leave of Perken and Claude "went back to savagery, like a bark towards a ship" (VR, p. 216). At Tcheng-Dai's funeral procession, banners waver "like ship masts." The participants in the procession create a "common movement that pitches and rolls like a ship"; numerous posters follow like birds following a ship (VR, pp. 127, 128). In *La Voie Royale* the carts bearing the precious sculptures roll jerkily through the forest "like barks on the sea" (VR, p. 130); the fatal pain in Perken's knee rises and falls "like a boat" (VR, p. 242).

In *La Voie Royale* Malraux employs the image of a boat hauler to describe Perken, as he advances towards the savages: "chest forward: a man without arms, his back bent like a boat hauler on stiff legs" (VR, p. 196). The analogy expresses not only a physical posture but something in the nature of a blind, unthinking courage. We find a similar usage, a rather melodramatic one, in connection with Hemmelrich, after the massacre of his family opens the way for him to fight with his friends: "Shoulders forward, he advanced like a hauler towards a vague place of which he knew only that people killed there, pulling with his shoulders and brain the weight of all his dead ones who, finally, no longer stopped him from advancing" (CH, p. 370). The image appears in a more simplified form in *L'Espoir* to convey the heroic efforts of men fighting for a just cause: "An enormous beam was just then moving forward like a geometrical monster, carried by fifty parallel men, bent forward like haulers, with or without collars, but all of them with a rifle on their backs" (LE, p. 464).

Boat imagery in *Le Temps du mépris* helps sustain the feeling of an unreal floating in isolation, during the early portion of Kassner's imprisonment. The music he imagines to himself pulls at all his wounds, "lifting him like a ship to a pitch of suffering"(TM, p. 52). He goes deeper into his dream world "in a long sweep of the sail beneath the wind" (TM, p. 56). A convent, in his hallucinations, becomes a "phantom vessel fleeing with the desolate clouds" (TM, p. 78). The tramping of imagined horses becomes the regular panting of a steamer; the horses are then pushed off course "like sails by the wind" (TM, pp. 79, 80).

Animals

The largest single cluster of all Malraux's images, and by far one of the more striking groups, is that of the animal world. Not surprisingly, it has been the object of the most extensive critical attention thus far devoted to imagery in Malraux's novels. G. O. Rees counts at least 350 instances of animal imagery.[2] My own count would revise that figure considerably upward, to something closer to 450 images in the six novels (still referring, of course, to instances of actual analogies, and not to the many additional references to animals at a literal level).[3]

Since it would be pointless here to state in detail what has already been clearly examined by Rees, our analysis of animal imagery can be limited to a brief summary of his major findings with a few additional illustrations and observations. His first group consists of animal analogies applied in various ways to human beings. They fix human portraits rapidly: Tchen looks like a hawk (CH, pp. 220, 308), Kassner has a horse face (TM, pp. 22, 23, 31), Möllberg's eyelids look like lizard skin (NA, p. 138), etc. They convey moral attributes and suggest character traits: Unamuno has the "noble, surprised, and pensive look of a graying owl" (LE, p. 752), the Vannec family feeds its gnawing dissensions like crabs that feed their parasites (VR, p. 31), and so forth. They render attitudes, gestures, movements, and sounds in human activity: children run, looking backward, like ducks (LC, p. 127), slow-thinking policemen become "cormorants crushed by thinking" (CH, p. 245), a crowd at a meeting approves of a speaker's remarks with the neck movement of barking dogs, and applauds by barking (LC, p. 110). The "spatial" quality of silence is brought out by figurative insect and rodent noises that lie beneath the calm (LC, p. 159, CH, p. 192, TM, p. 85, LE, pp. 690, 703). Rees might also have pointed out an opposite effect, the deadening of activity to create an unreal atmosphere, in several analogies to fish life and aquariums; these relate to crowds (CH, p. 265, LE, p. 797), amorphous groups of soldiers (CH, p. 371), dazed prisoners (NA, p. 16), hospital wards (LE, pp. 509, 511, 512, 514).

Rees's second group of animal analogies applies to inanimate objects. These are mostly commonplaces whose primary effect is to animate what would otherwise be static description. Houses seen from a plane look like a flock (TM, p. 130, LE, p. 817); bullets and shells fly by like flies (LE, p. 630), wasps (LE, pp. 488, 540), grasshoppers (LE, p. 447), pigeons (LE, p. 482); an isolated building "sits daydreaming like an ox" as it is being shelled (LE, p. 780). In the last three novels a more interesting pattern, pointed out by René Girard, but not by Rees, associates animal imagery with modern warfare, so that, through the image, the machine of war regains the terrifying aspect it once had.[4] Kassner's plane takes on the sensitivity of an animal (TM, p. 132), joins a storm in animal combat (TM, p. 134), is turned over by the storm like a whale turned over by a deep wave (TM, p. 138; for other such animal-planes, see LE, pp. 795, 823, 843). Bombed trucks lie on their backs with their "paws" up (LE, p. 518). The most recurrent such usage applies to tanks: they become protective turtle shells for the men inside (LE, p. 632), they move like enormous dogs (LE, p. 802), like horses (LE, pp. 737-38), lie on their backs with their bellies up when shelled (LE, p. 633), form an elephant graveyard when totally disabled (LE, p. 738). A trapped tank sticks its tail up like a certain kind of Japanese fish (NA, p. 274), is expected to turn over like an epileptic cat if shelled (NA, p. 268), finally starts moving again like a dying bull that gets on its feet (NA, pp. 283, 284).

The third of Rees's categories consists of animal imagery which renders ideas and emotions, images which are more subtle than the other animal analogies in that they support the major themes of struggle against humiliation, suffering, loneliness and death. The dominant image here is that of insect life, typifying the humiliation inherent in human existence, and found mostly in the humiliation of imprisonment. For Garine, humiliation in prison is embodied by larvae (LC, p. 46); for Kyo prisoners turn into worms, and provoke the same uneasiness as crustaceans and huge insects (CH, pp. 387, 389). The insect image appears no less than fourteen times in connection with Kassner's imprisonment: prison becomes a termite nest (TM, p. 103) filled with the swarming of invisible bugs (TM, p. 85), an anthill of little noises (TM, p. 37), where prisoners walk like tireless millipedes (TM, p. 45), where Kassner himself feels like a millipede stuck against the wall (TM, p. 60). Here, his guards' shadows turn into gigantic spiders (TM, p. 42), time becomes a black spider (TM, p. 61), code taps on the wall become ants that gnaw at time (TM, p. 96), "gathering" these taps turns him into a greedy insect (TM, p. 93), insomnia takes on the sharpness of an insect (TM, p. 88); and even when he is released, his spirit remains attached to his cell by a thousand spider webs (TM, p. 123).

It should be clear that literal imprisonment is only one aspect, a symptom, perhaps, of Malraux's concept of a greater human imprisonment, that humiliation is only one of several of what Rees calls metaphysical predicaments in the final section of his study—and that insect imagery is only the most obvious of a whole category of animal imagery whose function is to embody such predicaments. Malraux's novels are filled with animal imagery that relate physical and metaphysical anguish, affecting both the group and the individual. This can be illustrated most clearly by setting Rees's findings aside now to consider some of these predicaments.

In conjunction with masses of men, animal images—particularly those of suffering animals—highlight the degradation of human suffering: the masses eat animal food (LC, p. 103), look like ravaged beasts (LC, p. 144), become victimized herds (LC, pp. 10, 129, CH, p. 185, LE, pp. 797, 819). Prisoners become hungry animals in a cage (NA, p. 21), have catlike patience (NA, p. 26), run to their food like cats (NA, p. 20). Fish out of water depict the convulsions of a wounded soldier (LE, p. 504), the movements of fish mouths convey the suffocation of soldiers in battle (LE, p. 805) and the dazed state of prisoners (NA, p. 16). Insurgents are bowled over like rabbits (CH, p. 248); cries of the suffering and the dying turn into meowing (NA, p. 232), yelpings (CH, pp. 249, 244,, TM, p. 40, LE, p. 509), and sharp bird cries (NA, p. 273).

Applied to individuals, animal images can express both physical and mental distress. These are particularly frequent in *La Condition humaine*: Hemmelrich's love for his wife is expressed as that of a blind dog (CH, p. 312); his sick child looks like a skinned rabbit (CH, p. 332); May's grief is as poignant as that of animals; Gisors's obsession with death stirs beneath his love for art like the stirring of nervous dogs during sleep (CH, p. 229). The image can also characterize an individual's degradation: Clappique's intelligence is related to that of a sad monkey (CH, p. 320); this in itself does not reveal much, but after he sacrifices the revolution to his own mythomania, he goes home, grimaces at himself in a mirror, and is reduced to a monkey and a toad (CH, p. 372). His degradation is complete when, anxious to board a Europe-bound ship, he fervently wishes he were a dog so he could climb up unnoticed (CH, p. 397). These images represent Malraux's dominant picture of man, that of the victim; there is also the side of the persecutor, and this too is vividly rendered, if more rarely, through animal imagery. Leclerc's brutishness, for example, reduces him to an animal (LE, pp. 672, 682), and in particular a monkey (LE, pp. 476, 479, 671, 678, 684).

Faced with the prospect of persecution, men experience an anguish that goes far beyond grief to take on the proportions of terror. The terror of men in a prison yard, waiting to be executed, is depicted as inhuman (CH, p. 401), just as a man in a prison cell, such as Kassner, is apt to become subhuman (TM, p. 61). The most dramatic example of the inhuman-subhuman occurs in *La Voie Royale.* W. M. Frohock has noted that in this novel the jungle is identified with the frustration of human effort, that "shortly the insects come to represent the jungle," and that from a certain point "all the elements in the story which oppose the progress of Claude and Perken will be assimilated by metaphor to the insect."[5] What is particularly striking in this novel is the separate development of animal and insect imagery along two contrapuntal lines that intersect during the episode of Perken's bluffing the Mei warriors. Before that point, insects—literal and figurative—depict an exterior world of obstacle, culminating in an explosion of insect imagery applied to the waiting Meis (about eleven during the episode); only three insect images appear during the remainder of the novel. Animal imagery, before the turning point, most often depicts an interior world of uneasiness that applies to the two heroes, but gradually the reader finds himself in the midst of a great confusion of inhuman elements: the Meis are inhuman (VR, p. 151), subhuman (VR, p. 188); Grabot's inhuman presence strikes horror in the heart of Claude (VR, p. 174), his neck movements are those of a bull, his voice not human (VR, p. 181). Soon, terror reduces even Perken and Claude to a state of nonhumanity (VR, p. 191), until, finally, Perken works up enough sheer animal obstinacy

(VR, pp. 194, 195, 199) to face the savages. At the height of their confrontation with Perken, the Meis begin to lose their insect characteristics, becoming simply a herd (VR, p. 198) that Perken will subdue, and for the rest of the novel they will be depicted as terrified beasts, as nothing more than cattle (VR, pp. 236, 237, 249).

The image of the animal does indeed, as Girard points out, unite the animal to man, and thereby denies any optimistic doctrine of man's place in the universe because it attaches him to the cosmos from which he would be free (for a more balanced view, however, other image groups need to be taken into account). In the episode cited above, Perken does subdue the savages, but more through animal obstinacy than through a controlling human will. But a further distinction should be made: what most often unites Malraux's animals to men is distress and terror; the animal can react, but he cannot think, thus can oppose his persecutor only by brute force. The animal-human relationship in Malraux thus contains an ambiguity that may not be reducible to simple terms; for this weakness of animals, as applied to humans, frequently produces effects of endearing humor and even, strange to say, a tough but none the less tender pathos.

To be relegated to the life of an insect is clearly a fate far worse for Malraux than to have animal traits; it is, in a sense, more inhuman, not so much because the insect is savage, but because it represents that side in man which *blindly* submits to destiny, which in fact becomes a menacing element of that world which would bluff man into submission. The early novels abound in literal and figurative references to insects that buzz around lights, in submission to fate (VR, p. 158, CH, p. 295). Malraux characterizes terrorist groups—that is, groups ultimately committed to suicide—as a society of murderous insects (CH, p. 291). Literal flies appear in moments of confrontation with death, as a sort of physical embodiment of fatality: the narrator of *Les Conquérants* watches flies surround Klein's dead body, mosquitoes buzz in Perken's ears, flies land on a prisoner's face—and none of these characters seems to be able to brush away these anguishing presences (LC, p. 136, VR, pp. 259, 264, NA, p. 14). On the night of his first murder Tchen feels an insect on his arm which only turns out to be a momentary nervous spasm (CH, p. 182). Literal butterflies hover over dead men's faces (TM, p. 165, LE, p. 488), flies accompany Möllberg's disquieting discourse on man and underscore the nervous tension that precedes the release of poison gas (NA, pp. 129, 134, 157, 168); an ant crawls around the pistol with which Vincent's father has killed himself (NA, p. 91)—these are only a few examples of the insect's role as the embodiment of a fate over which man's will has no apparent force.

Prisoners live in humiliation, Meis live in savagery—but the insect imagery unites them in a common fate of submission to the nonhuman forces that seek to destroy all men. This greater predicament is an anguishing challenge to any concept of humanism, and Möllberg, in his devastating discourse, must feel a morbid sense of gratitude in being able to relate man to ants and termites (NA, pp. 130, 133, 149), and to refer to man's dialogue with culture as a dialogue between caterpillar and butterfly (NA, p. 148). And yet in his last novel Malraux will attempt to integrate all life—including insect life—in his search for the fundamental mystery of man. When Vincent Berger goes out into battle and sees animal, insect, and vegetable life poisoned, along with human beings—together the victims of some relentless drive in man to destroy—he will be impelled to find an antidote by exalting all life, and not just human existence. The presence of a live grasshopper and of straw and grass is somehow related to the rescue of the enemy soldiers. Malraux finally relinquishes the pejorative thrust of the insect analogy. For to get to the "fundamental" part of man, Malraux seems to have been obliged to get *behind* man, to the greater phenomenon of life; behind intellect and culture to a ground of sheer being. In this way Malraux allows his narrator to arrive at the desired sense of mystery and revelation needed to sustain the Pascalian observations on the double nature of man. Thinking of man's limited lot of happiness, the narrator writes: "Perhaps anguish is always the stronger part; perhaps it was poisoned at its very beginnings, this joy that was given to the only animal that knows it is not eternal." But he goes on to establish the dominant affirmation: "But, this morning, I am pure birth" (NA, p. 289).

Forms, Consistencies, and Miscellaneous Effects

Malraux frequently utilizes images of shapes as standard commonplaces for visual descriptions: a face is trapezoid (TM, p. 17), a line of tanks forms a crescent (LE, p. 731), etc. Several of these have to do with punctuation marks: commas and circumflex accents depict eyebrows and beards (LE, pp. 667, 698, 705), light effects on bowls form upside-down question marks just as Tchen declares his manifesto of terrorism (CH, p. 315); a movement forward takes on the shape of an *s* or *u* (VR, p. 238, LE, p. 821); a fire is "punctuated" by sparks (LE, p. 768), a voice by raindrops (NA, p. 96).

In considering light images we saw how Malraux can create dramatic effects by focusing attention on the center of triangles and rectangles of light, and set up confused masses that move between darkness and light by reducing objects and persons to shadows. These examples give evidence of two recurrent tendencies in Malraux's vision: one, to reduce observed phenomena to their bare skeleton, a clearly outlined geometrical form; the other, to swell and blur the shapes of those phenomena into amorphous, ill-defined masses. We are dealing here with the techniques of a visual art, at the same time painterly and cinematic. These are clear instances of synecdoche, the representation of a whole by one of its parts, and they are of interest to us here primarily for reasons of dramatic effect.

The effect of the rectangle most often is to create a disquieting void in which lurks a threat or the presence of death. It appears in connection with a number of dramatic scenes, for example the discovery of Grabot in his hut (VR, pp. 172, 176), the room in which Tchen commits his first murder (CH, pp. 181, 185), and the room in which Kyo lies dead (CH, p. 411). Circles and curves serve a traditional symbolic function of depicting a closed world of destiny. They most frequently apply to groups of people whose acts are controlled by higher powers: children (LC, p. 23), religious groups (LC, p. 63), beggars (VR, p. 70), prisoners (NA, p. 19), savages (VR, pp. 24, 178, 186, 205, 258).

Holes and tears, too, abound in the novels—they are, of course, circles in depth, windows that give onto nothingness. Images of circles, curves, and holes frequently interact to describe a predicament through movement or gesture: Grabot turns in circles around a mill (VR, p. 192); Kassner turns about his round prison cell, a geometrical void that is more than a trap—a hell (TM, pp. 31, 46, 51). Just before Tchen dies, everything seems to turn in large circles (CH, p. 354); shortly after, Clappique's roulette ball (we need not insist on a "wheel of fortune") will describe wide circumferences, fall into round holes, and thereby seal the fate of the Revolution. As Clappique finally leaves the Black Cat nightclub, Malraux writes in what one can assume to be consciously double-edged language, "le 'cercle' fermait" (CH, p. 361), where 'cercle' may be read as both club and circle.

Such images can constitute organizing structural motifs. At the beginning of *L'Espoir*, we see pigeons circling above street battles (LE, pp. 451, 453); as fighting becomes more serious, and battles become a war, the fighting shifts from Barcelona to Toledo, and it is planes that turn in circles (LE, pp. 518, 519, 555). When Tchen murders his first victim, he must make a tear through a mosquito net to reach the body; and what lies beyond that hole opens up an unknown world of destiny (CH, p. 183). Afterwards he goes to the window, looks up at a "tear" in the sky to see the stars which, as we have seen earlier, embody fate (CH, p. 184). Very shortly thereafter, Kyo and Katow look up at a tear in the clouds and see stars, and considerably later, just after the roulette episode, Clappique looks up, and through another tear and a hole, sees, not the stars but what is more appropriate for him, the moon (CH, p. 361).

The circle of fate can be broken by the straight line. The effect is frequently so subtle as to be scarcely noticeable: when Perken discovers poison spikes on the ground, he throws away his cigarette in a curving motion (VR, p. 150); shortly after, when he expresses the force of his will we read: "The red line that followed his shoulder moved: he had probably stretched out his hand. A minuscule gesture" (VR, p. 160).[6] Gisors, a man too old to act, still retains a fundamental virility that expresses itself through the voice, which takes on "the sharpness of a line" (CH, p. 209). Kassner's palm is generously endowed with a line of fate which he made himself with a razor (TM, p. 144). But Malraux's final depictions of the line relate, not to man's will, but to a nature which fulfills its own rhythm beyond human action. Towards the end of *L'Espoir* an apple tree rising above a circle of rotting fruit promises an eternal rhythm beyond man's transiency (LE, p. 835); the effect is similar when Vincent notices walnut trees rising above a circle of dead nuts (NA, p. 152); and Malraux's description of a flock of pigeons which fly in an arc, then break the arc to fly in another direction, contributes to the profound sense of reconciliation with a life that promises a multiplicity of possibilities (NA, p. 287).

Metonymic silhouettes function in the same way as shadows; that is, they reduce men and objects to dark, indistinguishable masses, filling scenes with brooding presences. There are no fewer than twenty-one of these images, most of which refer to groups of soldiers; "Silhouettes were hugging their rifles" (LE, p. 442); "Two silhouettes passed by merging in a pale halo" (NA, p. 201). There are even more metonymic reductions to spots (at least twenty-five instances), a distinctly painterly technique of accentuating bright areas against a darker background or vice versa. The more interesting of these rely on color identity: the light of the sun "plays above the edges of the sampans and brings out violently, from their brown backdrop, the women's blouses and pants—blue spots—and the children who have climbed onto the roofs—yellow spots" (LC, p. 56); "alternating spots—the black of tuxedos, the white of shoulders—bent over the green table" (CH, p. 357).

In a number of instances considered earlier, the quality of consistency or weight determines the expressive force of a vehicle—the lightness of clouds, dust, leaves, the solidity of earth, and so forth—these are only a few of a much larger number of images which are a characteristic feature of Malraux's style. As with images of form, the primary interest is that of an effect, a verbal or adjectival quality, rather than individual, substantive vehicles. One finds, for example, many images having to do with saturation and crushing weight. Although mostly commonplace in themselves, they become instruments for giving support to other presences and for creating a brooding thickness of atmosphere. Figurative saturation of one presence by another has the effect of loading the senses to uncomfortable surfeit. In *La Voie Royale,* the tropical silence is "saturated with moonlight" (VR, p. 136); in a harbor scene in *La Condition humaine* a night is "saturated with water" (CH, p. 195); a bay is "saturated with sunlight" (CH, p. 432). The image may give physical substance to an abstract idea or emotion, thereby conveying the strength and depth of an anxiety. Kassner is saturated with boredom in prison (TM, p. 97), Mercery with disgust while fighting an impossible fire (LE, p. 769), Vincent Berger with waiting to hear news of his father's death (NA, p. 36).

Images of weight perform a similar function of concretizing and overloading presences: electric lights in a hospital ward take on an "immobile heaviness" (LE, p. 800), a night is "loaded with a vague and limitless hope" (LE, p. 443). Tchen, considering the prospect of his own martyrdom, knows "with what weight blood shed for an idea weighs upon every thought" (CH, p. 353). The most recurrent such image has to do with crushing. The skyline of Hong Kong is "crushed by a cone of intense vegetation" (LC, p. 30), a voice in the jungle becomes "crushed by the vault of the leaves" (VR, p. 101), Tchen's night of murder is "crushed with anguish" (CH, p. 181). In *Le Temps du mépris* the image is applied to prison doors and stones as a material correlative for Kassner's spiritual condition (TM, pp. 44, 61, 101).

The largest group in this category of images of consistency has to do with decomposition: disintegration, rot, dissolving, dilution, and melting (together about forty-three instances). Their function is generally the same: in the context of an overwhelming predicament, they bring substantive embodiment to a collapse of human force and spirit, particularly in two of the novels. In *La Voie Royale*, as we have seen, they create a correspondence between the literal world of decay and the state of the characters, and together with images of crushing and saturation provide us with the most dramatic depiction in Malraux's work of the ultimate futility of the human defiance against the inhuman world. In *Le Temps du mépris*, the image most often takes the form of dissolving, conveying a deterioration in Kassner while in prison which, if allowed to continue, might have given us another Grabot. (Malraux's images having to do with fluidity, viscosity, stickiness, transparency, softness, and greasiness do not recur with any frequency and need not be considered here as having special significance.)

Malraux's novels are filled with abundant, detailed stage directions for background noises. The sounds of rifles and cannons, sirens, whistles, horns, telephones and radios, shouting and groaning, singing—a whole cacophony of accompaniment in scenes both of action and of contemplation—rise to crescendos and fade away into the background. Periods of silence are called to the reader's attention with the deliberateness of musical rests. Further, sounds are frequently echoed: a car horn echoes Clappique's rather hysterical laughter (CH, p. 298), guns echo a slap on the thighs (LE, p. 588), rain echoes hailstones falling on a plane (TM, p. 145), words echo an obsession (CH, p. 302), and so forth. The effect is one of prolongation, amplification—in short, depth. And it is likely that this same depth is what Malraux is after with his backgrounds of noise—it provides him with one further dimension, an auditory amplification, in the portrayals of the actions depicted. There may be symbolic effects as well. W. M. Frohock has pointed out that in *La Condition humaine* whistles become a symbol: they blow while there is hope that the insurrection will succeed, stop during its moments of difficulty, start again when the deaths of Kyo and Katow turn defeat into victory.[7] It is likely, as a general rule, that in all the novels the presence of loud noises is, of itself, a proof of action, hence a desirable state for Malraux's protagonists, and that silence, pure or broken by creeping noises, underscores an anxiety of waiting, fear, or hopelessness (notable examples, in addition to that of *La Condition humaine*, include the jungle silence of *La Voie Royale*, the prison silence of *Le Temps du mépris*, the poison gas episode of *Les Noyers de l'Altenburg*).

Malraux's analogies to man-made objects, although quite numerous, are primarily important for certain effects they achieve. Images of cloth materials, for example, appear very frequently from the first novel on as clichés for describing appearance: "curtains" and "sheets" depict bodies of smoke, fire, trees, fog, rain, and so forth. Malraux often likes to give his atmospheric presences of sky and clouds the flimsy consistency of shredded rags (*charpies, lambeaux*), and clouds can be "torn" like a curtain when bombs or a plane penetrate them. Images of paper fall into two types: the noise of crumpled paper may simply create a sound effect (see, for example, VR, p. 111, LE, p. 801, NA, p. 98), and paper's lack of substance may convey a notion of flimsiness as opposed to solidity (see, for example, LC, p. 29, LE, p. 489, NA, p. 235).

Malraux's need to express ideas and characteristics by reference to the solid or the hard is further served by analogies to tools. The image of a bar gives solidity to a number of entities: rays of light, fog, a river, a man's strength, and so forth (for examples, see LC, p. 84, TM, p. 132, LE, p. 568, NA, p. 193). Analogies to hammering and forging give substance to the marching of troops, explosions, even words spoken forcefully (LC, p. 161, VR, p. 89, LE, pp. 436, 780). Other images of tools and machines characterize a forceful or even violent attitude or movement: Garine's gesture of turning a screw underscores his hope to crush Hong Kong (LC, p. 62); a plane moves through a storm like a drill (TM, p. 137); smoke rises inexorably over a battle scene "with a mechanical regularity" (CH, p. 252), and so forth. Transportation vehicles, too, provide Malraux with a small source of imagery for characterizing motion: men advance like a car (VR, p. 81), a plane in a storm shakes like a delirious elevator (LE, p. 844); pushing back an assault is conveyed by analogy to a snowplow (LC, p. 57, CH, p. 263, LE, p. 453). Analogies to buildings, architecture, mirrors, cords, barrels, and a few others appear infrequently and require no special consideration.[8]

Notes

1. For an excellent study of dramatic highlighting and cinematic technique in Malraux's novels, see Jean Carduner, *La Création romanesque chez Malraux* (Paris: Nizet, 1968), Chapter 4.

2. G. O. Rees, "Animal Images in the Novels of André Malraux," *French Studies* 9 (1955): 129-42.

3. The variety breaks down as follows: about 90 refer to unspecified animals,

animal characteristics and activities, of which 6 relate to herds and 11 to the inhuman and subhuman. Of the named animals, about 41 refer to dogs, 25 to cats, 17 to horses, 12 to monkeys, 9 to rabbits, and lesser numbers to other rodents, bovines, frogs, wolves, etc., for a total of about 155 images. There are about 24 unspecified insect images, 11 that relate to flies and mosquitoes, 10 to ants, 9 to spiders, 7 to wasps, and lesser numbers to bees, butterflies, etc., for a total of about 99 insect images. Of the bird images, about 17 are unspecified, while 14 relate to various birds of prey, and lesser numbers to pigeons, sparrows, ducks, etc., for a total of about 70 images. Finally, about 12 images relate generally to fish and shell life, while 7 refer to aquariums, and lesser numbers to crabs, crustaceans, jellyfish, for a total of about 37 images.

4. René Girard, "Le Règne animal dans les romans d'André Malraux," *French Review* 26 (1953): 261-67.

5. W. M. Frohock, "Notes on Malraux's Symbols," *Romanic Review* 42 (December 1951): 274-81.

6. For a fuller analysis of Malraux's use of the hand and the straight line as breakers of the fatal circle, see the study by Albert Sonnenfeld, "Malraux and the Tyranny of Time: The Circle and the Gesture," *Romanic Review* 54 (October 1963): 198-212.

7. W. M. Frohock, "Notes on Malraux's Symbols"; cf. also Carduner, *La Création romanesque*, pp. 170-78.

8. For an extensive study of Malraux's attitude towards the world of nature, see Elizabeth A. Ellis, "André Malraux et le monde de la nature," *Archive des Lettres Modernes*, no. 157 (1975).

[3]

Imagery of Humanity

Animation and Personification

Malraux's world is suffused with a life which frequently cannot be thought of as being specifically human or animal, but a generalized force that permeates its object with attitude and movement. *L'Espoir* is particularly rich with objects endowed with life as a kind of response to what is happening about. Explosions cause windows to "moan" and tables to "stiffen," sirens to "throw" their call throughout an area; peace "spurts forth" from a fire; fires have their own independent life; and even a loudspeaker is described as "alive" because it talks (LE, pp. 507, 718, 721, 723, 743, 768, 803). These and numerous other examples underscore the tendency in this novel for events to take on epic proportions: played out against a cosmic backdrop, man's struggles with reality take on a grand and universal dimension.

But the interplay of the animate and the inanimate is a stylistic constant found not only in *L'Espoir* but in all Malraux's novels. The atmospheric presences discussed earlier are important for creating solid, nervous atmospheres which serve the author's purpose of objectifying the narrator's or character's awareness of human activity. But even beyond that, in Malraux's dramatic depiction of men struggling against the world, the world tends to become a character. In numerous instances we are not far from allegory; Malraux can speak of the "cry" of the earth, the "voice" of a storm, the "howl" and "voice" of pain, etc. (see, for example, VR, p. 183, TM, p. 82, LE, p. 508). Even Life itself is upon occasion personified: it can sweat, exchange glances with men, and be clasped in one's hands (LE, pp. 504, 644, NA, p. 285). Similarly, single objects may take on life to become active opponents to a character's designs. Such is the case, for example, with the stone sculpture that Claude Vannec must conquer and the roulette ball that takes on the force of fate for Clappique; both objects are filled with a living malevolence (VR, pp. 120, 124, CH, p. 360).

The inanimate world is frequently described, as well, as indifferent or passive. This kind of image is, of course, "romantic" in that it echoes a character's impatient desire for a close and favorable collaboration to be established between himself and the universe. Gisors' night is felt to be indifferent because he is anxious about Kyo's safety (CH, p. 227). Claude Vannec, impatient for his adventure to begin, finds his ship "passive"; and when night later falls over the jungle its "indifference" to his success almost stifles him (VR, pp. 58, 157). Clappique, frantically anxious to get passage out of Shanghai, finds the ships in the port "indifferent to him to the point of hatred" (CH, p. 396). Images of nonhuman indifference, then, serve Malraux as an ironic means of correcting the illusion of a friendly or hostile nature, depicted so abundantly in other images (see below), at the same time underscoring the anxious nature of his characters.

Communion and Noncommunion

The interplay between the animate and inanimate in any literary work can be of interest as it informs us of human attitudes. In Malraux such devices join an extensive body of imagery that define areas of communion and noncommunion. In *La Condition humaine* images frequently establish friendship between men and objects, but friendship between man and man usually finds a more direct, nonanalogical form of expression (indeed, sometimes quite lengthy). Tchen's only sure "friend," for example, is the force of darkness, Gisor's is the world of the opium dream, Clappique's at one point becomes the bric-a-brac of a bar (CH, pp. 187, 230, 298). The expression of love or desire for another person, on the other hand, generally comes across through some negated form. A marital problem turns the world of Kyo and May into one of hostility and alienation (CH, p. 328); Valérie's relation to Ferral is that of a stranger (CH, p. 265). Malraux in a few instances reduces the desired object to a synecdoche which he then personifies for ironic effect: Kyo sees a group of prisoners as a total "solitude and humiliation," and once Kyo dies he becomes Gisor's "dead hope" (CH, pp. 389, 413).

Communion and noncommunion in Malraux's novels are not merely themes, of course, but an essential dialogue, the very substance out of which the novels are wrought. Malraux's characters tend to perceive humanity in two general frameworks: that of the amorphous crowds that swarm through numerous scenes, embodying a universal anguish which the protagonists seek to redeem; and that of men organized into fighting groups by leaders for whom redemption means transforming that anguish into dignity—a dignity that justifies living. There is a gradual fusion of the two from the first novel, in which an image establishes Garine's disgust with a "fanatical crowd" (at one point he flatly states that he does not like people: LC, pp. 31, 45), to the later novels in which ordinary men are fondly recorded in their own impassioned accents. A striking example of the latter case occurs in *Les Noyers de l'Altenburg*: Vincent in his trench is surrounded by soldiers' voices which crystallize rapidly in his consciousness as a synecdoche for the entire

German people, then for just people, and finally for men (NA, p. 190).

The most evident key for observing this transformation through the novels is the image of brotherhood, frequently qualified as a "manly brotherhood" (*fraternité virile*). The sense of the image suggests the necessary steps that Malraux's characters must take to reach their ultimate goal: they must attach themselves to other people in love, and in a large sense identify themselves with these people. This love calls for a radical transformation in the character's notion of himself and the sense of his life. It means above all that he must undergo a process of liberating his imprisoned, introverted self in the name of a transcendental cause, which has to do with a notion of Man. The clearest examples of this liberation process probably occur in Malraux's characterization of Kyo and Kassner. Kassner's stay in prison, for example, can be seen as a symbolic statement of a condition of enforced alienation. At one point he feels that his sole "companion" is the throbbing of his own blood. But even this ultimate reliance upon his own identity cannot be assured; contemplating suicide, he suddenly feels estranged from his own hand. Once he is out of prison, a renewed process of identification with others takes place: danger will unite him and his pilot in friendship with all men then in danger. At the very end of the novel he exalts life and, through the eternity of life, "the only thing in man which was greater than man, the gift of friendship" (*le don viril*) (TM, pp. 77, 84, 129, 131, 184).

The images which express the imprisoned self take on a variety of forms, as we shall have numerous occasions to see in this study, recurring with particularly obsessive frequency in the earlier novels. The image of fraternity appears only once in the first novel, in the very last sentence of the book (LC, p. 162). In *La Voie Royale* it appears about three times, including, again, an important reference at the very end of the book (VR, pp. 226, 239, 268). From that point on, brotherhood is not merely an image but the essential antithesis to the thesis of alienation in the dialogue which Malraux will continue to elaborate through all the remaining novels.

One final pattern is worthy of note in connection with *Les Noyers de l'Altenburg*. In this novel, there are at least seven instances of imagery based upon friendly communion relating to an entity or force other than man. A walnut tree is "indulgent," a wind "faithful," the sun "benevolent" to the destinies of soldiers. The image of a gift appears three times in the latter portion to express the profound sense of awe in nature experienced by both Vincent and the narrator. When the narrator reflects that he seems to be seeing things through the eyes of a stranger it is not because he feels estranged but rather newborn. (NA, pp. 152, 181, 210, 284, 286, 290).

Women, Love, and Eroticism

Malraux uses the image of a woman to express characteristic features and gestures of men. Usually the effect is one of gentleness; such is the case for the painter Kama, the gallant soldier Hernandez, the philosopher Nietzsche (CH, p. 319, LE, p. 612, NA, p. 94). But in one case, in characterizing Nicolaieff's manner in *Les Conquérants* (LC, pp. 70, 157), the image serves a pejorative purpose. Nicolaieff turns out to be an inefficient revolutionary. A few other images of women—anonymous femininity and maternity associated with suffering—merely echo traditional role clichés.[1]

Malraux's love imagery is about evenly divided between the traditional man/woman relationship and erotic desires and sensations. These are fairly complex images. Of the first group, several are cast in a harsh mold. Most project a pejorative light on woman, all the while relating to considerations more important to the character than mere love. Tchen, for example, thinks of himself as capable of living with a woman who insists on possessing him, but is not certain he can live intimately with death (CH, p. 223). Another image of love, unusually brutal, confirms Tchen's propensity to think in terms of possession: not wishing to leave the assassination of Chiang Kai-shek to others, he tells Kyo: "I don't like for the women I love to be f——ed by other men" (CH, p. 290). Tchen frankly describes the woman's role in the sex act as one of weakness and humiliation (CH, p. 222). Just as characteristically, for Clappique the sex act is a form of suicide (CH, p. 364). In one image, bargaining becomes a kind of lovemaking; in another, love is merely the bait used by syphilis just as hope is a bait of war (CH, p. 306, LE, p. 852; see also VR, pp, 84, 85, 143 for other images of venereal disease). But making love can also be an analogy for experiencing life, and in particular express the experience of the profound change that comes over a man who discovers combat for the first time (CH, p. 188, LE, pp. 763, 848). Still, most of Malraux's love imagery relies upon traditional stereotyping that reflects in some way disparagingly upon the role or status of a woman who has relations with men.

The second type of image centers about erotic sensations. These define deep obsessions in some of the earlier characters in particular (it is useful to recall here that the earlier books have characters who need prostitutes: Garine, Perken, Ferral, and Clappique). Perken's desire to pit himself against his own death, for example, is likened to his desire for women; the exaltation he feels when exposed to the absurdity of life is like being in the presence of an undressed woman (VR, p. 87, 160-61). We find instances of sexual perversions as well. Nicolaieff describes the manner in which he interrogates prisoners with the smile of "a fat, old, excited man looking at a naked little girl" (LC, p. 96). After Valérie has taken her revenge on Ferral, this ostensibly iron-willed man indulges in masochistic fantasies with humiliated satisfaction and sexual pleasure (CH, p. 343).

The image of sexual desire is quite frequently related to the experience of danger in combat. For Perken, gnawed by a feeling of absurdity, to have erotic reflexes seems to prove to him that he is not weak but has the strength to impose his will (VR, pp. 192, 197).[2] For Claude Vannec eroticism is experienced when the will confronts death (VR, p. 55). Thus, when Kassner's plane begins to combat a storm, his senses are aroused "in a very precisely sexual way" (TM, p. 141). The narrator of *Les Noyers de l'Altenburg* states: "No name describes the feeling of marching on the enemy, and yet it is as specific, as strong as sexual desire or anxiety" (NA, p. 267). In short, the sex urge may be aroused when the hero is faced with a force that challenges his will. This fact alone would seem to bar a real flesh and blood woman from any effective action in the novels. In one episode that might be considered exceptional, Valérie almost succeeds in having her final say over Ferral, but Malraux allows Ferral to take his petty revenge by releasing birds to befoul her room. By the last three novels, literal and figurative eroticism has for the most part run its course.

Children and Childhood

The sheer number of images having to do with children and childhood (about fifty-four) and the presence of literal children, from the first through the last of the novels, gives evidence to an aspect in Malraux's work that deserves much closer attention than has thus far been granted in the critical literature devoted to Malraux. Indeed, the child motif may be one of the important keys for understanding an essential aspect of Malraux's thought. What follows is an interpretation of the child image that goes beyond a basic description in an attempt to give the material the emphasis it merits.

Malraux's analogies to children and childlike activities constitute a group of devices that are generally associated with contexts of anxiety and, as is frequently the case with these contexts in Malraux, a sense of disparity. In several instances the image expresses a sense of loss of face. Nicolaieff, an official interrogator caught derelict in his duties, nervously sweeps dead moths off the top of his desk "with the gesture of a well-behaved child" (LC, p. 158). Leclerc returns from a flying mission without having unloaded his bombs and offers bad excuses "like a child caught jumping over the fence" (LE, p. 670). The anxiety here is obvious; the disparity stems from the fact that these are normally tough men, not given to behaving like children. In other instances the image colors thought in a more subtle manner. Captain Wurtz, for example, who is something of an initiator into warfare for Vincent Berger, asks Professor Hoffman a question on the effects of poison gas; the professor answers in the cold language of scientific precision, and we read: "Wurtz gave a clumsy smile, like a gigantic child who has done something wrong" (NA, p. 178). Wurtz, too, is normally a tough man, but using poison gas on the enemy is an idea he cannot cope with very well; so that the image sustains the general feeling of an essential innocence in the face of something monstrous.

During the Altenburg discussion Möllberg poses a basic question in the following terms: "We must determine if our civilization, as the best minds in Germany are proclaiming today, carries within it the human past just as a man carries within him the child that he was" (NA, p. 141). His argument will lead to a negative response: the "human adventure" is not an adventure but a metamorphosis, men of one age or culture cannot truly be said to communicate with those of another, and the notion of fundamental man is an intellectual's fiction. Yet Möllberg does not actually confirm or deny the second term of his analogy, the existence of a significant relationship between a man and the child that he was. He actually obscures it somewhat when he states later: "I doubt that there is a dialogue between the caterpillar and the butterfly" (NA, p. 148)—as though a consideration of a purely morphological nature were sufficient to dispose of the problem.

To judge from Malraux's elaborations on the man/child theme, recurrent in all the novels, we may surmise that the author has in mind a refutation of Möllberg's pessimism with regards to the central issue. There *is* a significant relationship between man and child, and in the very romantic sense that an uncorrupted state of innocence and naiveté lies beneath the mask of mature men. In a few instances this truth is expressed as a surprising discovery. Hong's smile, for example, "bares his teeth and suddenly gives his hate-filled face an almost childlike expression" (LC, p. 101); and in *L'Espoir*: "When Vargas raised his brow, he took on a naive look, and suddenly seemed younger; and Magnin noticed that he had never thought that Don Quixote could have been young" (LE, p. 528). More often the image is stated as a general truth wherein the sense of disparity has been assimilated through reflection. Claude Vannec studies an old photograph of Grabot, the mysterious adventurer: "He knew these faces upon which a child's expression reappeared beneath the brutality of man, in his laugh, in his eyes rounded by surprise, in his gestures" (VR, p. 154). Here there is no anxiety, no reaction of surprise or shock, but rather a sense of never-ending wonder about man.

This sense comes out forcefully in certain privileged moments, in particular when a man is facing danger or undergoes suffering. The face of Kassner's pilot takes on the look of childhood: "it was not the first time . . . that, as he looked on, resolution in danger plastered upon a man's face the mask of his childhood"; Mireaux's face, after he is wounded: "there, suffering had gone to find childhood" (TM, p. 139, LE, p. 832). A reflection of Kassner's provides an even sharper insight into the idea that holds a number of these images together: "Only the approach of death gives one the right to perceive in a man the childlike mask he had just witnessed" (TM, p. 140). This comes remarkably close to a romantic expression of man's duality, the kind of transformation we associate with Dr. Jekyll/Mr. Hyde, or the picture of Dorian Grey. Malraux's man, too, is by his very nature an ironic creature, but the dichotomy is structured along lines that differ from the romantic ones of good and evil. To the visible eye he is a tough, virile activist, one who has chosen sides and taken on a role, often a dark creature enveloped by the hard shell of extreme experience, and hence something of an impenetrable mystery for all other men. At heart he is an innocent, impressionable child, capable of basic and uncomplicated joy and sorrow, pure of contamination by his role or past experiences.

In *L'Espoir* the American journalist Shade makes the following comment as he watches ex-Fascist soldiers troop by to fight for the Republicans: "There is something I like here: men are like kids. What I like always looks like kids, close up or from afar. You look at a man, you see the child in him, accidentally, you're hooked . . . . Look at them: they are all bringing out the child within them that they usually hide" (LE, p. 469). As child, man is no mystery at all—he shares his basic humanness with all other men, and is open to communication with them. Indeed, Malraux's principal form of communication among men is, as we have seen, a "manly brotherhood," where the phraseology itself suggests something of the spirit of childhood and adolescence wedded to the adult man.

From the first novel progressively to the last, Malraux's sentimental bias towards men seems more and more to embrace *all* men, the heroic as well as the unheroic. *L'Espoir* is the novel in which the notion of a "fundamental" man begins to take on the importance of a major theme; it is also particularly rich in revelations of the child in man. Karlitch, pleased to see that his machinegun operations will go well, "burst into a sharp, rather childlike laugh"; Moreno: "On this perfectly regular mask, every profound feeling appears as a childlike expression"; "Nadal, a small, squat boy, with curly hair and almost mauve eyes, would have made a possible gigolo if everything about him had not been too round: his face, eyes, even his gestures which were too circular, matched his tightly curled hair in an almost childlike way"; Heinrich: "the back of his neck was shaved smooth, and a thoughtful pout made his old, polished face look childlike" (LE, pp. 496, 624, 673, 776). In the last novel, the quest for a fundamental man becomes a predominant preoccupation of both Bergers, father and son; but while in the father's case a revelation is expressed through a marveling at the tenacity of natural life, in the son's case it comes through child and birth imagery. His three tank mates all reveal some aspect of the child within them. Bonneau, the "tough guy," once lets his "terror" mask fall, revealing "his soul, incurably infantile"; Pradé lives exclusively for his eleven-year-old son. Once the four men have fallen into the tank pit they are overcome with terror, and at some point in this inhuman trap their essential nature comes through: Bonneau's face trembles like that of a child "waiting for a couple of slaps"; it "has taken on in the presence of death something horribly innocent." Pradé's face, like Bonneau's, becomes "innocent," and he states with a grim smile as he identifies with his son, "The kid—this time, I think he's had it." When they think they have succeeded in maneuvering the tank out of the trap, it is Léonard's "childlike" voice that announces the good news. Subsequently, in the barnyard where they have found refuge, the narrator will describe his feelings several times, as we have seen, in terms of a birth; and even the world seems reborn: "With its trees branching out like veins, the universe is as full and mysterious as a young body" (NA, pp. 261, 276, 280, 290).

The dichotomy spoken of above is also one that distinguishes between energy and form. Möllberg is not wrong because of an incorrect argument, but because his formalistic approach is not sufficient to cover the mystery that had earlier on plagued Vincent's uncle Walter. The narrator writes:

> "From one lost day to the next, I am more and more obsessed by the mystery which does not, as Walter affirmed, oppose but rather connects, through a barely visible link, the formless side of my companions to the songs that hold up against the eternity of the night sky, to the nobleness that man does not know is in him—to the victorious side of the only animal who knows he is going to die." (NA, p. 250)

Man and child are not two mutually exclusive terrains. Rather, one contains the other; the material forms may differ but the spiritual energy is continuous. While it is not in the scope of this study to pursue fully Malraux's treatment of Möllberg's argument, the implication should be clear: one civilization can communicate with another, not because of the myriad forms with which it envelops itself, but despite them, through the essential, universal, and eternal energy which we call human and which, as in the case of the child, can open itself upon the world many times and still rediscover that world.

There is, in the novels, yet another sort of analogy to children, associated with reactions of anxiety. Malraux's characters are visibly susceptible to the suffering of children, and generally feel helpless before it. Allusions to children, at a literal level, abound in the novels; Malraux notes, for example, the presence of children as factors of misery in crowd scenes, the harming of children as an instrument to incite revulsion, the legendary heroism of men who have brought aid to children, the reflections of fighting men on their own vulnerability towards children's helplessness (see, for example, LC, pp. 90, 100, 105, CH, p. 243, LE, pp. 450, 689, 799, NA, p. 131, 164). Even as tough a young rebel against society as Claude Vannec, who feels nothing but scorn for men who submit to the order of things, makes an exception for the man who has children (VR, p. 54). For Kyo, about to die in the prison yard, the sacrifice of the prisoners who surround him becomes all the more poignant when he reflects that "like Hemmelrich, almost all these men had children" (CH, p. 406). But it is the image of a suffering child that most clearly exposes the raw nerve of the characters' vulnerability. Garcia reflects on Guernico: "This defenseless body moved him as children moved him, because it denied any idea of combat." When Schreiner fails his flying test, after so anxiously wanting to pass it, the other pilots move away from him "as though from a dying child, as though from any disaster for which human words are paltry" (LE, pp. 691, 494).

Is there any reason that can account for so preponderant a preoccupation, other than the author's own possible vulnerability to a child's helplessness? Again, certain of the images provide insights. Kassner, in prison, busies himself with preparing an imaginary speech to his comrades: "There are a few men who turn their thoughts to us as if we were their dead children" (TM, p. 108). Attignies tries to describe to Magnin the ties that bind communists to their party despite the errors of the party: " 'If your child is wrong, do you hold it against him?' 'Yes. But if your father is wrong . . . . ' 'I didn't say your father, I said your child" '(LE, p. 567). The child is obviously conceived of as a bond among men, a very treasured one. For if it is true that men can succeed in communicating effectively at the profoundly interior level of the child within them, then that child must be safeguarded as a last hope. When the bond that unites Kyo and May is threatened, the image of a sick child appears: "This often taut love that united them like a sick child, the shared sense of their life and death, this carnal understanding between them, nothing of all this existed in the presence of a fate that fades the forms with which our sight is saturated" (CH, p. 214). But this moment of extreme despair is mastered when Kyo considers that the bond still holds—and that it *must* hold: "With her alone I share in common this love—

broken or not—as others share, together, children who are sick and may die" (CH, p. 219). The image mirrors the literal presence in the novel of Hemmelrich's sick child, an impediment to the father's joining actively with his fellow insurgents. With the death of that child, Hemmelrich will enter into the last combat of the novel, less for ideological reasons than for revenge against the forces which destroyed his last hopes. May, too, at the end of the novel, will probably manage to assuage her grief in accordance with Gisors's last words: "On the road to revenge, my little May, you encounter life" (CH, p. 432). And yet these words strike one as containing some bitter irony, as does the entire concluding section of *La Condition humaine*; for Gisors also states: "May, listen: it doesn't take nine months but sixty years to make a man . . . . And when that man is made, when there is nothing left in him of the child or of the adolescent, when he is truly a man, he is only good for dying" (CH 432).

When a man loses the child within him, or the literal child outside him that sustains the inner one, then that man is nothing but a shell. The implications go far. The dichotomy in Malraux's man does not oppose good to evil, but rather the will to act to the outcome of action, the capacity to rediscover the world to the acceptance of fatality, the innocent vision to the fossil of accumulated experience. This dichotomy is perhaps most clearly seen in Malraux's distinctions between the spirit of the "conqueror" and the role of the "guardian." The dilemma Malraux's protagonists encounter over and over again takes on existential proportions: the desired goal of kinetic action leads inexorably towards the static, finished act, just as becoming can lead to being, and life to death.

The child in man is not only the channel of communication between men but the very stuff of his individual passion, the source by which he preserves his power for self-renewal. In the introduction to *Le Temps du mépris* Malraux has a bone to pick with Flaubert, who used Art to create characters alien to the author's own passion, and who could write of them: "I shall roll them all in the same mud." He counters Flaubert's outlook with a formulation that assimilates the fictional experience of his characters to the predominant role of the creative process itself: "One may wish art to mean an attempt to inform men of the greatness within them of which they are not aware" (TM, pp. 8-9). This mysterious greatness in man is profoundly related to the child every man carries within himself. When Kassner returns to Prague after his release from prison, he experiences a profound jolt. In the hell of prison he had consumed all the energies of his mind to stave off an impending madness, and his senses had virtually died. Now as he walks alone before the shops of Prague, his senses come back to life and his imagination is set into motion upon contact with the great variety of bric-a-brac of modern civilization exposed in the shop windows; and simultaneously, the factor of childhood appears: "His sharpened senses bestowed upon the dazzling window-shop jumble, as he passed by, the fantastic quality of the spectacles created by his imagination when as a child he would come out of his fairyland worlds" (TM, p. 147). After the surrogate death in prison, Kassner is reborn through the child within him who leads him to the rediscovery of life, through the power of an imagination that transforms one reality—the ordinary, static one—into another, marvelous reality in which everything becomes possible. What Malraux means by "greatness" in man cannot be easily defined, but the impetus to greatness clearly lies in man's capacity to sense the marvelous and to renew the self; and that capacity is conveyed by the image of the child.

Time, History, and Culture

Stories have always had to deal with the problem of time; that time should be more than a technique but an obsession is more typically modern. Malraux's novels can be seen as adventures against human time in search of historic time—and they are served by a fairly considerable body of images that relate to time at a number of levels. The most frequent sources are the seasons, the past, prehistoric time, a returning to present time, clocks and watches, and eternity.

These images fall into several areas of interest. Seasonal time is perhaps the least significant—leaves falling during a battle are a fairly commonplace representation of autumn and death (LE, p. 729); images of a summer atmosphere in the woods and a "definitive" autumn help dramatize the spectacle of an exterminated life in the poison gas episode of the last novel (NA, pp. 221, 225). Images of suspended time serve the more important function of conveying an anguished impatience, and references to the mechanism of watches and clocks further dramatize an awareness of the self seemingly frozen in eternity. There are several such moments in *La Voie Royale.* Spiderwebs in the jungle seem to hold daylight in an "immobile eternity." When a small notch is made in the face of the stone sculpture that Claude is eager to secure, dust spills out with the slowness of an hourglass. Oppressive jungle noises strike Claude as a "solid alarmclock" ticking away with precision against the silence of the inhuman world: "This tick-tock attached Claude to the life of men through its persistence, its sharpness, its invincibility which belonged to any mechanical object." When the two adventurers are trapped by the savages, it seems that "time alone was alive, crushing, in this deserted place: the minutes were prisoners of this circle of brutes which was taking on a character of eternity" (VR, pp. 99, 124, 159, 186).

In *La Condition humaine* the revolt in Shanghai stops time so that even street lights emanate "a sordid eternity"; an essential moment of communion between Kyo and May is "rotted by passing time" because Kyo's committee is waiting; Clappique tries to hide his watch from Gisors, after failing to meet a scheduled deadline that could have saved Kyo's life, "as though the watch had betrayed him" (CH, pp. 192, 329, 374). In the last novel, the "indifferent noise" of a travel clock in the room in which Vincent's father lies dead, and an ant crawling on a revolver which his father had not had to use (the strychnine had worked), fill Vincent with a sense of anxiety: "Mechanical and alive like this scratching noise, the order of insect communities stretched across the world beneath a mysterious human freedom" (NA, p. 91).

Malraux frequently plunges back in time to apply his image. Just before Tchen commits suicide, our eyes are directed to Chinese signs: "the enormous characters faded into this tragic and hazy world as though into the centuries; and, as though it too had come, not from military headquarters, but from Buddhist times, the horn of Chiang Kai-shek's car began to sound" (CH, p. 353). The effect here is to place Tchen's Occidental act of terrorism into a distinctly Oriental perspective of fate, to suggest that Tchen's outlook on life and death is fundamentally an Eastern one. At the very depth of the past lies prehistory, an era that provides Malraux with no fewer than thirteen images. These allusions can establish a strange, unreal, morose kind of atmosphere. The jungle for Claude, for example, is a "beginning of the world" setting (VR, p. 99). During battle scenes in *L'Espoir*, tanks and even a skyscraper take on the proportions of prehistoric beasts (LE, p. 592, 633, 694).

The back and forth movement in time stands out particularly sharply in one of the final episodes of *L'Espoir*. At one point in that novel Alvear tells Scali: "The age of the fundamental is beginning again . . . . Reason must be *founded anew*" (LE, p. 705). Alvear's prophecy bears fruit towards the end of the novel. Magnin must lead an expedition through the mountains of northern Spain to find a downed plane, but the trip becomes, as well, a voyage into a primeval past, in which man and nature are reduced to a fundamental existence. As the trip begins, Magnin enters a hostile landscape, an "eternal" Spain (LE, p. 826), but though the way is hard, the outcome is successful: Magnin finds his men, brings them down in grave dignity through "ageless" mountain gorges (LE, p. 835), encounters the tender concern of a woman who becomes an incarnation of "eternal motherhood" (LE, p. 835), and of a whole village that follows the wounded downhill with the same sort of expressive compassion as we find in *La Condition humaine*, where the fraternal anguish of condemned men follows Katow to his execution. But this time the journey is to life and, as we have seen, it is significant that this promise of human life through common dignity is framed against a lone apple tree rising above a ring of rotting, but germinating, fruit, which comes to represent an eternity beyond human life and death (LE, p. 835). The music Manuel hears at the very end of the novel becomes something "graver than the blood of men, more disturbing than their presence on earth—the infinite possibility of their destiny" (LE, p. 858).

Malraux's imagery of history and cultures covers a wide range. From the realm of archeology and ancient civilizations there are about twelve images, of which three relate to Babylonia, three to ancient Peru, three to mummies (Malraux's interest and knowledge in archeology is, of course, quite well known; one might recall at this point that two important characters, Garcia and Möllberg, are ethnologists). We find thirteen images relating to the Near East, thirteen to Asia, eight to Africa and Negroes, eleven to American Indians. From Western history, there are four images of Rome, two of Huns, two of Vikings, eleven of the medieval period; seven images are specifically Spanish, seven Mexican, thirteen French, sixteen of modern Europe; and finally, there are a few other images relating generally to history, politics and races. This rather impressive body of imagery is related to another important group having to do with visual arts and literature, which for practical purposes will be treated separately.

Of the images that relate to people, a large number give

us rapid portraits of individuals and groups, with no probable intention other than rendering a visual likeness. Some of these portraits are based on racial and national similarities: peasant horsemen look like a Mongol tribe (LE, p. 539), Scali has the face of a mulatto (LE, pp. 477, 546), Hong's laugh resembles that of a Negro (LC, p. 25). Several characters look like American Indians: Jaime (LE, p. 465), Vegas (LE, p. 492), Enrique with his "totem" profile (LE, pp. 561, 564), and likewise Malraux's only two Americans, Pastor Smithson and Shade (CH, p. 301, LE, p. 596). Another group of visual portraits is established on analogies of historical and cultural types: Clappique's grimaces before a mirror transform him into a carnival samurai (CH, p. 372), Magnin looks like an astonished Viking (LE, p. 479); Manuel's normally Roman face becomes, when unshaven, that of a Mediterranean sailor (LE, p. 481); a Mexican militiaman is depicted several times as "the Terror of Pancho Villa" (LE, pp. 591, 599, 600). Still another group of portrait imagery relates to individual historical figures: Pradas looks like Mazarin and Lenin (LE, p. 596), Gérard like Czar Nicholas II (LC, p. 12), Frenchmen fighting in Spain like Thorez and Maurice Chevalier (LE, p. 666).

Malraux's cultural portraiture frequently serves the more elaborate function of depicting moral attitudes and character traits: Claude's grandfather dies with the heroic dignity of an old Viking (VR, p. 32), a Spaniard responds with the gallantry of one of Charles V's captains (LE, pp. 457-58), militiamen dispute with the stupid futility of cab drivers in the streets of Paris (LE, p. 595). Not all the attributes are heroic. The look of a Nazi guard, for example, resembles that of a slave buyer (TM, p. 87), and tribal desert khans look either like patrician Moslem warriors or else like rug merchants (NA, p. 69).

Images with a political thrust appear quite frequently. Organizational communists are spoken of as being of the "Roman" type (LC, p. 150). The "romantic" style of the

Spanish insurgents, depicted in the earlier portion of *L'Espoir,* is likened to that of the Mexican Revolution and the Paris Commune (LE, p. 500). Lopez expresses a desire to see a new style of painting born in Spain similar to the revolutionary mural style in Mexico (LE, p. 472). In another image, men grouped around a cannon look like an engraving of a scene from the French Revolution (LE, p. 464); and there are several instances in *Les Conquérants* and *L'Espoir* of analogies to the French Revolution that illustrate some of the problems encountered by characters in these two novels in pursuing their own revolutionary plans (LC, pp. 15, 18, 106, 148, LE, pp. 455, 855). As we might expect, there are also images that set up feelings of anxiety: the song of Asiatic caravan drivers twice depicts an intensity of anguish that derives from a knowledge of death (CH, pp. 287-88, LE, p. 535); men in predicaments are transformed into shriveled, petrified Peruvian mummies (NA, pp. 25, 282-83), and so forth.

Another major category consists of imagery established through an analogy to specific geographical landscapes. The effect may be simply visual: the Teruel battle front is shaped like the Malayan peninsula (LE, p. 815), a store front is as variegated as Red Square (TM, p. 20), the skyline of Hong Kong under its tropical vegetation is strangely like that of London or Hamburg (LC, p. 30). These are the kinds of images that might come to the mind of anyone acquainted with maps and pictures. But there are other images, particularly those of Asia, sufficiently specific or remote from the tenor of the image to be the probable fruit of an experienced reality (since most of them occur in the last novels, they might also be the fruit of elaborated memories). These include some of Malraux's most vivid descriptions of decor and atmosphere. The dry Spanish landscape is filled with a "Mauritanian" solitude (LE, p. 477), is dotted with "Kurdish" villages (LE, p. 826); cadavers in Toledo make that city smell like Asiatic swamps (LE, p. 587). Several of these analogies set up a weird decor strangely divorced from the violence and suffering depicted simultaneously: the lights of Hong Kong, seen from a ship, transform that modern city into a strange "Polynesian spectacle" (LC, p. 30); a hospital rises up above a battle area like a Babylonian tower (LE, p. 780); and twice the Indian technique of *trompe-l'oeil* decor conveys the unreal atmosphere of battles in Spanish towns (LE, pp. 587, 851).

Mysticism, Religion, and the Bible

Malraux frequently expresses the notion that men are controlled by external forces with images of gods and sacrifices. Tcheng-Dai, for example, is obsessed with a "god" of Justice (LC, pp. 67, 57, 68), and Tchen's act of murder is expressed as a sacrifice to propitiate the gods of the revolution (CH, pp. 181-82). Clappique's roulette ball is a god to whom he sacrifices that revolution (CH, p. 359); later he experiences a feeling of self-sacrifice to the Europe-bound ships which become intercessors of an unknown god (CH, p. 346).

Two corollaries develop from the imagery of controlling gods: men are not like gods, and men must be delivered of gods. The first idea subjects man to a feeling of rancor against the gods, envy for them, or quiet resignation, for a condition which deprives him of unlimited freedom (CH, pp. 349-50, LE, p. 616, NA, pp. 28, 140). There is only one such image of God: Vincent Berger claims that art is a stylization of an object "such as man would have created it if he had been God" (NA, p. 128). The second appears as a need for a new order in which man's will replaces the gods (CH, p. 426), and as admiration for the Greek sculptor who initiated such an order (NA, p. 98). The images thus support one of the major themes of Malraux's novels, the polarity of fate/

free will, expressed by several other types of images as well.

The depiction of an abstract fate is frequently supported by mysterious signs, powers, and prophets. *Les Noyers de l'Altenburg* alone contains a dozen images of this type, so that no reader of Malraux's last novel is likely to miss the point that he is dealing with an adventure cast quite deeply in a mystical mode; this we shall examine shortly. But the other novels are not devoid of an irrational element, and offer a certain number of analogies to mystical signs: omens (CH, p. 263, LE, p. 488), fetishes (LC, p. 68), revelations (VR, pp. 200, 228-29), prophecies (VR, p. 25), trances (VR, p. 232, CH, p. 275, LE, p. 593). Tchen's "passion" very clearly identifies him as a mystic (CH, p. 340). Images of rebirth appear several times. As early as *La Voie Royale* Malraux has Claude state that the artist has the power to resurrect (VR, p. 61). Significantly, the same power is endowed on Pei's journalism (CH, p. 353): he wishes to resurrect political martyrs; and presumably the same may be said of Malraux's conception of his own goal for at least his third, fourth, and fifth novels.

A wide variety of figurative demons, monsters, and spirits, too, populate the novels. Hong sees in misery a kind of smooth-tongued demon determined to prove man's depravity (LC, p. 104); but for the most part these images add a fantastic note on a grand scale, imparting a legendary tone to real activity. Tanks, for example, are not only demons (CH, p. 205), but monsters (NA, p. 288); a battering ram is seen as a geometrical monster (LE, p. 464), a mattress stuffed with family possessions becomes a monstrous giant (CH, p. 235), and smoke from jungle fires advances relentlessly like legendary genies (VR, p. 239).

Malraux's religious imagery covers extensive ground, including universal concepts such as prayer, specific Catholic rituals and institutions, and the Bible. A number of the analogies serve to characterize an individual's visual or moral aspect. Shade, for example, resembles a Breton priest

(LE, p. 469), Kama has an ascetic's face (CH, p. 320), Tchen looks like a hawk "converted by Francis of Assisi" (CH, p. 220), Vincent Berger has the prudence of a Papal nuncio (NA, p. 51). Images of the clergy bear a pejorative allusion in the first novel: a priest's unction characterizes both Tcheng-Dai and Nicolaieff (LC, pp. 60, 70, 77, 116). Other images focus on church objects for visual effect, but these have an invariably grim, ironic content. A machine gun dominates a setting like a tabernacle (CH, p. 370). Warring factions meet, but leave a "holy" space between themselves (LE, p. 594). Four men against the wall of a tank trap form "a single cross" (NA, p. 281). Children's hearses are as ornate as communion cakes (LE, p. 796). Clichés associated with the Church appear a few times. The manner in which men or explosives fall, for example, is described in *L'Espoir* as a rosary chain (LE, pp. 451, 728, 780), the ritualistic repetitions of masses of followers are expressed as litanies (LC, pp. 71, 109-10, LE, p. 757). Clichés of hell also appear, but a specifically Dantesque Inferno can also be found: Perken, in his most dangerous encounter, recalls hell's punishment for pride (VR, p. 192); for Garcia, watching the enormous fires of Madrid, men's lives "turn along one small infernal circle" (LE, pp. 764-65); Bonneau is a bully who places all his victims in one infernal circle (NA, p. 255).

On the whole, then, this imagery performs its functions without necessarily injecting a religious note into the novels. In terms of mystical hope or spiritual renewal, we might recall here the general sense that each of the novels conveys. The first two novels, despite the grand deeds depicted, end with a sense of futility and solitude; the presence of a witnessing spectator—the narrator in *Les Conquérants* and Claude Vannec in *La Voie Royale*—suggests a possibility of transcendental communion, but that is not developed. In *La Condition humaine*, the Revolution itself becomes the new religion of triumphant human will that replaces religious fatalism (CH, p. 426); and yet hope is quite tenuous. As the insurrection begins, Tchen senses invisible crowds animating this "Last Judgment" night (CH, p. 193); the fact that one city, Hankow, has been taken by the Left transforms the city into a "Promised Land" (CH, p. 263). At the end hope is expressed through the imminent rebirth of martyrs who will shed more blood, if need be, in the name of that cause. Just before he dies Kyo reflects on good men outside the prison who turn their minds to the condemned heroes "just as believing people pray" (CH, p. 406). But hope in the cause is also tempered by grief. Gisors's suffering at the death of Kyo becomes "the only prayer that his dead son's body could hear" (CH, p. 414).

The fourth novel, *Le Temps du mépris*, ends in a kind of hope tempered by grave sorrow. The fate represented in this novel is by far the most crushing in all Malraux's novels: there is simply nothing substantial that the human will can oppose to the prison experience. Kassner's obsession of escaping continues "his subterranean life, like eternal salvation beneath the sinner's life of a Christian" (TM, p. 68). The fact that he will eventually be released is thus virtually miraculous, and every experience he will go through subsequently will nourish a growing faith in him, despite all the odds against victory. At the end Kassner experiences "one of those moments that make men believe that a god has just been born" (TM, p. 183).

L'Espoir provides us the first occasion for the possibility of an *actual* victory, in the name of human dignity, through concerted action. Here again the Revolution is the new religion in which the Communists, now in a pejorative light, take on the role of "priests" (LE, pp. 704, 603). Here we find "end of the world" imagery (LE, pp. 761, 803), and the expression of an Apocalypse which is no longer just an illustration for something else but an elaborate program (LE, pp. 530, 532, 609, 843). At the end there is little emphasis on the necessity for further bloodshed; Manuel, who dominates the concluding pages, sits at an organ to fill a church with "the voice of the other world" (LE, p. 848), in accompaniment to speculations on the ever-renewed possibilities of human destiny.

At the end of *Les Noyers de l'Altenburg*, spiritual hope does not take the form of martyrdom or even further action, but rather of mystery in the rebirth of life itself. A consideration of most of the imagery having to do with time, history, culture, mysteries, and religion in this novel has thus far been postponed in order to illustrate how these images, taken together, are not merely useful devices but a basic structural rhythm that informs the essential meaning of the book. The central portion of the story recounts three episodes in the life of Vincent Berger. The first relates his T.E. Lawrence-like career in the Middle East. He is an adventurer who is frankly described as a Shaman (NA, p. 49). In Central Asia he had hoped to rekindle the flame of Islam in the name of a Pan-Islamic myth; instead he finds that "the God of the burning bush was nothing but ritual" (p. 70). He finally realizes that he has failed to see that the myth is nonexistent, just as "before Luther innumerable fervent Christians had come to Rome without seeing the simony there" (p. 71). The second episode centers about his attendance at the Altenburg conference. Between these two episodes we read of the strange sensations he experiences upon returning to Europe. For a moment, he cannot completely separate his recent Asiatic experience from this rediscoverd Europe: women's new fashions make them walk like Chinese women with their tight steps (p. 76); the people of Marseilles seem as strange as the forlorn Asiatic tribesmen he had encountered earlier. An so, thrown "upon some shore of nothingness or eternity, he contemplated the confused flow" (p. 78). In another image, Vincent explains his sensation to himself as one of being freed from time (p. 92)—and combined with the inexplicable event of his father's suicide, he realizes he has discovered man's capacity for noncontingency, the possibility that he can be released from the fatality of historical *and* personal time; therein lies what Joseph Frank has called Malraux's intuition of the "sacred."[3]

This strange discovery reverberates in Vincent's mind even during Möllberg's systematic exposition of man at various stages in a primeval past, which will lead to the conclusion that there is *no* human adventure, and that history has no meaning. Vincent's intuition of noncontingency might also have taken this pessimistic turn—the recent shock of encountering two cultures (Asiatic and European) and two time spans (Europe before and after his departure) might well have led him to conclude that there is no unity to history. But, as we have earlier seen, the presence of walnut and the spectacle of the tenacious life of nature come as a revelation. Stieglitz had previously stated that the Middle Ages is an eternal present (p. 140)—Vincent's intuition informs him that there is a unity to history because things continue, because, therefore, there is an eternal present, moved by a secret which he is only now beginning to understand, and which he will explore in the third episode.

Vincent soon discovers in his battle trench on the Russian front that the men about him have been reduced to a common humanity faced with a common enemy. Men's voices fill the "primitive darkness" (p. 190), and Vincent hears, not individual Germans, but Germans, all men, of all times: one soldier has a Moslem style lock of hair (p. 202), helmets look like Saracen caps (p. 212), their common fear of the enemy dates back to Saturnian times (p. 211). They speak of mysteries with a voice that makes Vincent suspect "how childlike the voices of sorcerers of long ago must have been" (p. 194), and read their fortunes in tarot cards (p. 210). Further, as they talk of their old trades back home, he suddenly wonders if it is the men who are speaking or the trades themselves (p. 196)—trades which have an *eternal* existence beneath impersonal and provisory men (p. 199). These men that Malraux has unified through references to history, culture, and ageless activities will undergo an instinctive experience together; they discover that the *real* enemy is not the Russians, but their own poison gas, which becomes a prehistoric monster (p. 207), filling the battlefield with a prehistoric silence (p. 232), striking the area with "a Biblical punishment" (p. 234), destroying men who are "friends of Quaternary men" (p. 243). Finding a poisoned Russian soldier, Vincent is filled with panic: "believers probably call this visitation of fright the presence of the demon. The Spirit of Evil here was stronger than death" (p. 233). Coming back into an unpoisoned area is like finding a "valley of the Promised Land" (p. 230). German soldiers rescuing the Russian enemy animate death "with a secret life" (p. 234); matter seems to be reborn in straw, creating a new, but still the same, race of animals and insects (p. 242). The entire episode, encompassing death and life, murder and communion, is presented as a dazzling Apocalypse (p. 243): one group of men who have no ostensible reason to feel related to another group, will none the less be moved by a secret attraction, an invisible bond shared with them, that must ultimately be related to a process of identification with the most fundamental part of man.

These significant experiences in time and history will be rediscovered and relived in a more condensed form by Vincent's son, the narrator of the novel, in the two episodes that frame Vincent's adventures. The book opens with a scene laid in a medieval church, the Cathedral of Chartres, transformed into a Nazi prison camp for French soldiers, men who are still dazed with battle and capture, immensely tired, and, in effect, stripped of everything but an essential humanity faced with very basic problems of individual survival. And here in this camp removed from contingent history, where a fence can be "Roman," shacks "Babylonian," and a tired voice "prehistoric" (pp. 24, 25, 26), the author finds in the faces of the bearded prisoners a common bond—they all have "Gothic" faces, and they walk about the area like medieval beggars (pp. 17, 25, 28). In short order, the narrator has depicted the feeling of noncontingency and, through a series of medieval imagery, placed in the context of a medieval decor, has established an eternal present at the point of origin of an unbroken line of European history. The prison compound has become a world of mystery. Their prison guards become oracles who give instructions in prophetic intonations (pp. 15, 17); their steaming pots hold witches' soup, and their bread becomes manna (pp. 19, 23).

The concluding frame repeats the third of Vincent's experiences, a descent into hell—this time by means of a tank trapped in a field being shelled by the Germans—followed by a similar joyous revelation of the mystery of life. And once more the narrator plunges figuratively into the past, through the buzzing of centuries (p. 287), to rediscover a Gothic age of miracles, of myths of animals that speak, of men who invent a watering can, to close his book on a note of revelation and resurrection through a vision of eternal life (pp. 286, 287, 288, 290, 291, 292). The narrator has moved out of the darkness of death into the revelation of a Biblical dawn (p. 291); tanks then become monsters drinking from Biblical wells, barns belong to Paradise, and the narrator suddenly understands what gift the Three Wise Men brought to Jesus and the pleasure of God upon beholding the first man (pp. 288, 290, 292).

The Body: Blood, Hands, Eyes

Malraux's analogies to the human body and bodily activities are generally striking through some unexpected, frequently negative, quality. Several parts of the body (the nose, the brow, the face, flesh) are employed with sporadic frequency, and require no further consideration. By far the most important of Malraux's body images have to do with blood, the hands, and the eyes. Malraux's blood imagery tends to fall into two kinds of patterns. In one his use of heart beats, blood pulsations and palpitations, and veins reflect the charged presences of frenetic, chaotic activity—the hidden heartbeats of human life. Tchen thinks of Shanghai, for example, as a city that "palpitated with the trembling of a lurking multitude" (CH, p. 192); in *L'Espoir* a city filled with footsteps quivers "like a vein" (LE, p. 690). But these are only external symptoms of a more interior condition. Malraux's characters can often be found listening to the beating of their own heart, the pulsating of blood through their veins and temples, sometimes in accompaniment to the joy of communion or to the awareness of man's potential greatness, but more often as a symptom of anxiety. Kassner and the unknown prisoner in his neighboring cell listen to each other's secret signals "as they might have heard the mute beating of their joined hearts" (TM, p. 100). But Kyo reflects while in Hankow: "Anxiety is a strange feeling: you sense by the rhythm of your heart that you are breathing badly, as though you were breathing with your heart" (CH, p. 277). Images having to do with sweating, breathing and panting perform a similar function: people "sweat" anxiety (LE, p. 795), prison walls "sweat" destinies (TM, p. 38), thoughts "pant" like breathing (CH, p. 316), a whole room breathes together (NA, p. 134), etc.

A second group of blood images centers about the violence of bloodshed. The amount of literal blood that flows freely through Malraux's novels is impressive. Spots of blood are liberally sprinkled through the first five novels, as signs of the presence of violence and death (there are at least ten such references in *La Condition humaine* alone). The loss of blood means death or near death. For several characters it becomes a striking figure for expressing the fear of losing control over the will or hope. Garine speaks for a number of the action-obsessed characters when he states: "When my action splits itself off from me, when I begin to split myself off from it, it's also blood that is being lost" (LC 143). Claude's sense of frustration in the jungle is expressed as a feeling as if his blood, "beat by beat, were draining out" (VR, p. 124). Kassner waits for a knock from the neighboring cell in his prison, but hope leaves him "like the last false wave of blood expelled from a wound by the irrepressible beating of his heart" (TM, p. 66).

But in *L'Espoir* the emphasis shifts from the individual flowing of blood to the blood link. Blood is the fraternal bond of good men. The men in Spain fighting against Fascism are "the blood delegated by half of the proletariat of Europe" (LE, p. 713). Once Manuel has established military leadership over his men in *L'Espoir* we read: "Manuel exchanged, with one after the other, these glances that concluded a blood allegiance with him" (LE, p. 773). Bloodshed is also natural, as opposed, for example, to death by torture, burning, or poison gas (see LE, p. 790, NA, p. 232). It is the price everyone knows he may have to pay to achieve dignity. Yet when, at the end of *L'Espoir*, Spain has been bled completely dry, a new phase begins, and consciousness turns away from death: "Spain, bled dry, was finally becoming aware of itself—like someone who suddenly questions himself at the moment of death" (LE, p. 858). Significantly, there are no images of this type in the last novel.

Malraux's characters have busy, revealing hands. We are constantly watching men who extend their hands, shake hands with each other, give active force to ideas by gestures of the hand and fist, seek fraternal union through touching and joining of hands. Involuntary motions of the hand disclose insecurity anxieties better than words: a woman spy keeps wiping her hands before her interrogators (NA, pp. 162-64), Gisors keeps rolling imaginary cigarettes (CH, pp. 221-226), Manuel must always carry a stick of some sort until he no longer needs a prop to his confidence (LE, pp. 731-848 *passim*). And, of course, men kill with their hands.

A few of the hand and arm images Malraux employs to indicate comparative size and to create visual and tactile effects. But the great majority of them are related in some way to the function of the hand as the instrument of the will, the challenger of destiny. England's imperialism, for example, is described as a thief's hand that must be cut off (LC, p. 129). Grabot is a living proof of Claude's eventual destiny, hence Claude considers shooting him for a moment, "like a killer who cuts off his convicting finger" (VR, p. 186). The hand embodies the need to crush, to seize, to possess and hold firm. Perken, for example, speaks of his desire for a woman, and Claude guesses his gesture in the dark: "like a hand that crushes" (VR, p. 90). Gisors's hands, when he talks, seem "to seize something" (CH, p. 209). Once he is together with his wife, Kassner seems "to seize their eternity" (TM, p. 183). Malraux's characters often underscore their words by pounding fists and raising a pointed finger; there are even purely figurative movements of this type. Barca, in *L'Espoir*, speaks slowly "with the tone that he would have used if, seated at a table, he had raised his index finger" (LE, p. 513); in the tank pit, Pradé's voice takes on an accent "which seems to underscore everything with his fist" (NA, p. 263).

The hand is quite clearly symbolic, then, of the very process by which Malraux's characters take on their being—the need to act, to impose the self upon reality. The correlation is so clear that Malraux on occasion focuses on attention on a disembodied hand as a metonymic bearer for the shaper of destiny. When Katow gives his poison to a fellow prisoner, he does so "to this warm hand that was touching him, not even to bodies, not even to voices" (CH, p. 409); the prisoner will thus have the final satisfaction of executing himself through his own will rather than die in torture at the hands of the enemy. The lines in Kassner's palm express directions on the surface of the earth. His life line is naturally long, but his fortune line is the result of a razor cut: "In this way had been made all the lines that marked his own destiny, not by a razor cut but by a patient and tenacious will; what was human liberty other than the awareness and organization of one's fate?" (TM, pp. 144-45). When Kassner arrives in Prague he studies a shop window in which gloves on display seem to become active hands, symbols of man's renewed hope (TM, p. 148). Malraux underscores Perken's final sense of anguish by suspending action to allow for a prolonged consideration of Perken's hand. This hand, which had performed his acts and shaped his world, had lost its power to feel and now becomes an alien object. It represents the loss of his past achievements, of his will—so that his literal death simply climaxes the psychological death of a man who realizes the vanity and impermanence of his power (VR, pp. 262, 263, 265, 266, 267).

But if the hand represents an individual man's capacity to shape destiny, it also embodies man's call to brotherly communion. This motif appears as early as the first two novels, in the final paragraphs of which, as we have seen, references to brotherhood appear. Garine removes his arm from his sling in order to embrace the narrator (LC, p. 162). Claude embraces Perken, as if to "express with his hands and his eyes, if not through words, this desperate brotherhood" (VR, p. 268). In *La Condition humaine*, there is a dramatic depiction of a human chain formed by men with one will and one instrumentality; a chain in which Tchen, however, senses that he is an unreliable link (CH, p. 254). Even Katow's gift of poison, in the final analysis, represents a gift of immeasureable love: he is sacrificing his individual need to allow a weaker friend to express *his* will.

Malraux's interest in the eyes and eyesight most often takes the negative form of violence to the eyes and blindness. Together with a fairly copious body of images related to the eyes, the many references to real blind men establish blindness as one of Malraux's more important themes. Blindness becomes a major motif in *La Voie Royale*, for example. Here we find a description of a blind musician, who hypnotizes a circle of dancing girls into a kind of delirium, associated with Perken's erotic obsession (VR, p. 13). A blind reciter of the Ramayana, encircled by a group of beggars and servant women, evokes the decomposition of human culture in the midst of ruins. The association of blindness with a circle is a significant one, and can be compared with Malraux's association of the outstretched hand with a straight line; one represents human fate, the other human will. Perken recounts how Grabot had deliberately infected one of his eyes as an act of defiance (VR, p. 93); when Perken and Claude discover that Grabot is totally blind we have at the same time the depiction of an ironic justice meted out to an overly defiant man as well as a closing of the circle of fate. In the village where Grabot is imprisoned there is a blind slave (VR, p. 166); and, of course, when we see Grabot he is turning in circles about a mill, so that the total effect has the air of a Greek heroic tragedy taking place in the Indochinese jungle.

Literal blindness is important in *L'Espoir*, too. Jaime's blindness is a constant reminder to his comrades of their own potential destiny (LE, p. 682). During the course of the war, Madrid seems to have been invaded by blind men (LE, pp. 690-95 *passim*). At the very end of the novel, Manuel will recollect seeing one of these blind men, his hands outstretched in a light which makes them seem "as long as the hands of destiny" (LE, p. 858). An image in *Les Noyers de l'Altenburg* renders the sense of these images more explicit. As Vincent studies the medieval statues in this hall filled with intellectual debate, we read: "Greek statues look towards the inside, thought my father, but the handsome medieval ones always look like blind men who are searching . . . . Like these men who surrounded him, the prey of the demon of an intelligible world . . . ." (NA, p. 144). What Malraux may be saying is that the Greek artists who created statues understood that the true search for understanding must be conducted *within*, while modern Western man, from the Middle Ages on, seems doomed to spend his life searching outside for something that will forever elude his grasp. The motif occurs already in Malraux's first novel, *Les Conquérants*, when Garine is summoned to witness the body of Klein, one of his most faithful—and humane—followers. Klein had been tortured before being killed, and his eyelids have been cut off, so that the whites of his eyes stare blankly, and permanently, outward. Garine, reflecting upon the meaning of this omen shortly afterwards, recalls the anecdote of an emperor who had the eyes of his prisoners blinded, and had them led home by one-eyed guards who eventually become totally blinded as well, and he concludes that this is "just the right storybook picture to express what the hell we are doing here" (LC, p. 138). At the end of *L'Espoir*, Manuel will reflect: "He felt life about him, swelling with omens, as though, behind these low clouds that the cannon no longer shook, blind destinies were silently waiting for him" (LE, p. 858).[4]

Malraux's images of blindness characterize, with obsessive recurrence, the futility of action and the sense of helplessness that crush men in moments of despair. Connoting a closed world of darkness, the image is an effective device for expressing the sense of claustrophobia that overcomes the solitary man—or the man who cannot communicate. Moreno, in *L'Espoir*, says: "They say that being blind is a universe; being alone is one too" (LE, p. 625). As long as Claude Vannec keeps his plans for adventure to himself, he is "cut off from the world, tied to an incommunicable universe like that of the blind or the mad" (VR, p. 57). It can depict the inability to understand or perceive; Claude describes museum pieces as objects, "and we are blind before them until our myths relate to them" (VR, p. 61). It expresses the archetypal fear of darkness and the unknown that several characters share in their search for light and awareness; Garine says ominously of his darkened house: "I can't get used to this darkness; it always makes me feel like I'm blind" (LC, p. 159).

Distress, Violence, and Death

All of Malraux's novels deal with heroes who live in a state of antagonism against various forces, physically real ones as well as metaphysical and psychological enemies. There are no novels in which literal contexts of physical distress, violence, and death do not abound. Indeed, most of the episodes are embedded in these contexts, and as one might expect there is a quite considerable body of imagery that depicts the individual and universal manifestation of a world gone wrong.

These images are based upon a fairly wide variety of sources. Malraux's images of physical distress take the form of generalized weakness or specific states including intoxication, hunger, fevers, colds, tuberculosis, leprosy, cancer, gangrene, the plague and nausea. His medical imagery, not particularly abundant or well defined, requires no special consideration. Analogies to physical disabilities relate to wounds, sores, scars, amputations, paralysis, muteness, and hunchbacks. The images of violence include torture, execution, drowning, strangling, smothering, poisoning, burns, accidents, the hunt, and various forms of physical blows. Finally, there are images of the ultimate enemy: figurative suicide, the death agony, cadavers and skulls, funerals, and the presence of death itself.

Since all these images are related in nature, and perform essentially the same tasks, they can be considered together here. Some of them illustrate abstract notions. Garine's plan in *Les Conquérants*, for example, is to destroy Hong Kong "as surely as a cancer" (LC, p. 54). Both an early and a later hero in the novels, Perken and Vincent Berger, are obsessed with the idea of "leaving a scar" on the earth—an image that embodies the recurrent theme of leading an active, aggressive existence.

A number of these images create visual effects. A man crouches as though wounded in the stomach (LE, p. 585);

roads and canals from a plane look like scars (TM, p. 144); Spanish villages look like burns on the landscape (LE, p. 826). Garine, suffering from some fatal illness, takes on the look of a cadaver, and his head is like a skull (LC, pp. 33, 60). Others create sensuous effects: a guard's whip strikes like a hook (CH, p. 391); a flame-thrower repels a soldier "like a kick" (LE, p. 544). As is the case with so many of Malraux's images, they frequently personify inanimate entities: a truck shifting gears sounds like a wounded machine (LE, p. 482); the uncompleted steeple of the cathedral of Strasbourg seems to be amputated (NA, p. 152). Death, in particular, is endowed with animate characteristics in quite a few images, and takes on the force of an allegory: death is attentive (LE, p. 568), has a voice (CH, p. 275, NA, p. 279), can wait for higher orders (NA, p. 194), arrive (LE, p. 831), warn men (NA, p. 279), select its victims (CH, p. 243), approach them (CH, p. 384), hide behind their backs (NA, p. 93), crouch in their hearts (TM, p. 165), and seize them (VR, pp. 267-68). Cities can die, and lights look cadaverous (CH, p. 288, LE, pp. 519, 640, 694, 723, 856).

Still other images characterize manners and attitudes: wounded prisoners lie as though paralyzed (NA, p. 16), and coolies sleep outdoors in Shanghai "in plague-stricken attitudes" (CH, p. 296). Lying in prison, Kyo assumes "the position of the dead" and Kassner unwittingly brings his feet together and crosses his hands on his chest, "like a corpse" (CH, p. 405, TM, p. 50). Clappique, whose mythomania inherently entails a perpetual suicide of some essential personality, applies the image of suicide to himself to characterize his obsession with gambling and eroticism (CH, pp. 360, 364-65).

The content of all such images clearly communicates the inherently tragic or violent condition of man and the universe. When Hong, in *Les Conquérants*, describes the life of the poor as a long torture (LC, p. 101) he is in essence giving one form of expression to a universal human condition. All

Malraux's characters, in one sense or another, belong to the world of the miserable simply by being alive. Kassner believes that the conditions for living, for example, make it inherently unlikely for the victim to be stronger than the executioner (TM, p. 35); and Perken, as he lies dying, realizes that life itself is the executioner (VR, p. 262)

It is significant, therefore, that while Malraux's characters are given abundant opportunities to commit literal violence, his images most often establish man as the victim, not the persecutor. Antagonists such as enemy soldiers and prison guards, usually nameless and amorphous, seem to be nothing more than agents of destiny. In one image, they are merely the "indifferent delegation" of a personified Torture (TM, p. 63). Identified antagonists such as English imperialists, Chiang Kai-shek and Franco are usually not even seen at all. When they are—for example, the Mei tribesmen—they have already been reduced to a nonhuman form of existence. Malraux describes these savages as looking like hunters, yet Perken will see in them only a symbol of his own humiliated destiny; when he finally dies, his real "hunter" will be the light of the sun (VR, pp. 192, 205, 265).

Malraux's characters are victims, and the imagery depicts them in their suffering. The suffering is frequently simple physical pain. Advancing through the jungle Claude feels as though his arm were being pierced by "the needle of a doctor who had once, while poking clumsily at his vein, scraped his flesh" (VR, p. 101). More often it is depicted as a generalized state of grave sorrow. When Kassner finally comes face to face with his wife, he gives "a paralyzed smile that he felt stretch the skin of his face like a wound that closes over" (TM, p. 169). There are instances, too, that communicate a sense of the grotesque. Grabot asks Claude Vannec a question, and "the despair of a mute" seizes Claude (VR, p. 174); wounded soldiers howl "with the strangled cries of half mutes" (CH, p. 253); Hemmelrich becomes fascinated by everything about "to crush him like a coffin lid screwed over a living man" (CH, p. 385). In the last two novels, where the Earth becomes important in its own right, the suffering and violence apply to the nonhuman as well. Several images of "gutted" houses and buildings in *L'Espoir* describe the effects of fires and bombs (LE, pp. 733 ff.). In the poison gas episode in *Les Noyers de l'Altenburg* a prolonged sequence of images having to do with purulence, vomit, the scourge, and reactions of disgust and nausea, dramatize the transformation of the natural world into rot (NA, pp. 208, 218, 223, 226, 231, 242).

Malraux's characters suffer psychologically as well as physically—indeed, the obsessive depiction of states of anxiety one finds in the novels make Malraux one of the most visible writers of *Angst* in all French literature. The images of distress and violence can give concrete weight to states of simple nervousness. The movements of a captured pilot, for example, are like those of a nervous tubercular (LE, p. 549); a woman spy being interrogated keeps changing her tone "as if she had been slapped" (NA, p. 163); the anxiety of soldiers in a battle trench does not disappear but thickens, "like a critical illness that become chronic" (NA, p. 184). These images apply with particular force to a characteristic state of nervousness one finds in all the novels: having to wait. The narrator of *Les Conquérants* reports that "as soon as we wait for something, we rediscover the heat, like a wound" (LC, p. 88). Kassner realizes in prison that he must endure patiently, "like the paralyzed, like the dying, with this stubborn, buried will" (TM, p. 46). Soldiers in *L'Espoir* become anxious for battle to begin so that they can end "this waiting of the sick" (LE, p. 484); pilots on the ground, waiting for a long overdue plane to return, begin to lose hope, which "struggles like someone smothering" (LE, p. 476). Clappique places a bet in a gambling room, then watches the roulette ball spin "as he might have waited after swallowing a poison" (CH, p. 360).

In the same connection, images of intoxication appear

with some frequency. In the first two novels, a state of figurative drunkenness applies to the young initiates, eager to get on with their missions (LC, pp. 41, 42, VR, pp. 17, 57). In certain of the characters, an insatiable desire for satisfaction is expressed as being overwhelming as in a state of intoxication. Perken, crushed with a sense of futility, is drunk with the desire to destroy a prostitute through sheer strength (VR, pp. 232); König's appetite for killing communists is like that of opium smokers (CH, p. 379). Clappique becomes drunk with his lies—his mythomania is in fact a virtually literal form of intoxication (CH, pp. 364, 371, 380). In the latter novels, however, images of intoxication suggest, simply, complete saturation, with no pejorative connotation: Kassner is drunk with humanity, soldiers with their sense of brotherhood, and so forth (TM, p. 152, LE, p. 609).

Such images, as we can see, are often associated with a sense of hopelessness that penetrates men when they become aware of the obtuseness of reality. Images of hunger and nausea similarly depict a powerful sense of frustration. Perken, obsessed with the passage of time, feels emptied of hope with a force that comes over him "like hunger" (VR, p. 89). Later, when he understands that his jungle empire is crumbling, he experiences an anxiety "like those semilosses of consciousness that precede vomiting" (VR, p. 242). Kyo, in prison, senses his powerlessness before the prison guard "to the point of wanting to vomit" (CH, p. 388); and as he witnesses the torture of a prisoner, he senses the same horror as a "student in medicine the first time that a stomach opened in his presence shows its living organs" (CH p. 390).

There are images, too, that depict another recurrent form of anxiety in the novels: the sense of alienation. One sort is the feeling of being shut off from the world of men. Kassner in prison reflects that even if he should get out "he would discover upon leaving a world forever amputated, he would carry this solitary death like a scar" (TM, p. 48). Vincent

Berger, on the other hand, who had thought that his long stay in Asia would "amputate" him from Western culture, has no difficulty in rediscovering it (NA, p. 121). At the end of *La Condition humaine* Gisors's face appears to come back to May "from the depths of death, as alien as a cadaver in a common grave" (CH, p. 431). A more insidious kind of alienation, found principally in the earlier novels, has to do with feeling split off from oneself. The famous episode in *La Condition humaine* in which Kyo fails to recognize his own voice on a record finds Kyo struggling "with the same complex uneasiness with which, as a child, he had looked at his tonsils, that the surgeon had just removed" (CH, p. 198). Three of the "conqueror" types in the early novels are likewise quite lucidly aware of their peculiar schizophrenia. Garine characterizes himself by allusion to a strange ceremony in which two men, one live and one dead, are tied together. Perken, who learns that he may die, is "at the same time chained to his flesh and separated from it, like those men who were drowned by tying cadavers to them" (VR, p. 226). Ferral discovers in sleep, beneath his various masks, his only reality, "this joy of abandoning oneself, of leaving on the shore, like the body of a drowned companion, this being, himself, whose life he had to reinvent each day" (CH, p. 351). The opposite effect, that of returning from a state of alienation, likewise finds expression through similar imagery. After Claude Vannec succeeds in securing his stone sculpture, "the world came back to him as to a drowned man" (VR, p. 127). Tchen leaves the scene of his murder and contemplates the ordinary world of men "as a cured blindman looks, as a starved man eats" (CH, p. 185). When Kassner finds Anna again, after his ordeal, her face slowly comes back to him "as someone who has fainted comes back to life" (TM, pp. 176-77).

Garine, who is literally ill, associates illness with existence itself; it is his identity: "People think that it is something against which you struggle, an exterior thing. It isn't: sickness is one's self" (LC, p. 108). Seen as an interior state, illness clearly connotes the inherent weakness of the human condition; it implies the ever constant threat of failure and death. Hence it can dramatize—especially for the earlier, victory-obsessed heroes—a loss of courage. When Claude momentarily gives in to his sense of frustration, he imagines that his arms are pressed tightly against his chest "as in a fever" (VR, p. 124). Perken, finally forced to face up to a line of savage warriors, thinks he will die in "this leprosy of courage that had destroyed Grabot" (VR, p. 191); without his gun his empty hand goes limp, "as light as a sick man's hand" (VR, p. 197). Garine explains that the poor are doomed to remain, without courage, in their misery: "they dissolve in it as though they had leprosy" (LC, p. 144). And yet there is one of the poor, Hong, who has courage, but perhaps precisely because of his background his courage has become so extreme that he is now a terrorist: "He thinks of his life like a tubercular who still has all his strength, but no hope" (LC, p. 105).

The image of illness may thus connote a peculiarly privileged state of awareness of a dilemma—privileged because only a few persons have truly apprehended the absolutely inflexible order of fate, which is that every man must die. The reaction, as one might expect, is one of hostility. During the Altenburg dialogues, Möllberg answers someone who has disagreed with him "with the mute violence of the incurable who has heard his illness imprudently mentioned by someone" (NA, p. 148). Claude Vannec would rather pit himself against death than "accept while alive the vanity of his existence, like a cancer" (VR, p. 55); and Perken knows that time is developing in him "like a cancer—irrevocably" (VR, p. 158). This state of awareness can be shared with others who also understand, for Malraux's characters evince a kind of instinctive attraction to another person who is about to die. At the literal level, we have clear examples of this attraction at the end of the first two novels, where one character watches another about to die with brotherly concern. There are examples at the figurative level as well. When Kyo and May go into their marital crisis, Kyo finds himself in front of her "as before a dying person; and as towards a dying person, his instinct threw him towards her" (CH, p. 216). Hemmelrich is obsessed by Tchen "as by a dying friend." Sharing the awareness of death is thus a means of binding men in intimacy. Claude recalls that his grandparents "shared in their lives a tacit hostility, like invalids sharing their infirmity" (VR, p. 27). Manuel discusses his "moral drama" with Ximenes, who has gone through a similar crisis, just as "a sick man chooses to discuss death with another sick man" (LE, p. 775). The image of women in labor pains, similarly, unites wounded men who share their suffering. During a battle scene in *La Condition humaine*, Malraux writes: "The guttural howl of a woman in labor passed across the moans which started again like an echo" (CH, p. 253). When the wounded in a hospital, in *L'Espoir*, stop howling, Manuel hears them grinding their teeth, "like the cries of women in labor" (LE, p. 509).

Prisons, Barriers, and Enclosures

Literal presences of walls, barriers, and barricades appear frequently in the novels, serving as backdrops, like the sky (see Chapter 2), against which a dramatic action can take place, or as labyrinthine lines to enclose an action (see, for example, CH, pp. 187, 309, 401, 403, LE, p. 581, NA, p. 70). These features of decor provide images as well. The image of a closing door can depict the anguish of a lost hope. When Kyo leaves May, closing two doors behind him, she waits anxiously "as if she expected a third, nonexistent door, to close in its turn" (CH, p. 329). Kassner's prison door, as it closes on him, "crushes" him (TM, p. 44). When, on the other hand, at the end of *Les Noyers de l'Altenburg* the narrator rejoices in literal "half-opened doors" we know that he has discovered the realm of hope (NA, pp. 290, 291).

The image of a closed space can render a feeling which is stated literally in one instance: "closed spaces make anxiety more intense" (LE, p. 756). As Kyo, worried about the outcome of the insurrection in Shanghai, walks along with Katow, he "plunged into himself as into this alley which became darker and darker" (CH, p. 218). Kyo and Tchen together in the open night feel as close as if they were "in a closed room" (CH, p. 288); Manuel's uneasiness in a closed room depicts his emotional state as he enters a street filled with snipers (LE, p. 635); and the presence of a Fascist army around a city is felt "like a presence in the darkness of a closed room" (LE, pp. 697-98). By communicating a sense of anxiety and claustrophobia, these analogies thus take on the expressive function of the prison image.

Literal imprisonment is, of course, a recurrent predicament in several of the novels, an experience shared by Garine, Grabot, Kyo, Kassner, and several groups of soldiers. These literal experiences are richly served by vehicles of a number of categories. But in addition imprisonment itself is a recurrent vehicle in the novels (there are over forty instances), and together with the related images of barriers and enclosed spaces such as traps, walls, closed doors, blocked alleyways and courtyards, and so forth (there are over thirty of these) they constitute an image group of some significance. The effect of the image is visual in only a few instances: bars cover closed business establishments as though they were prisons (LC, p. 31, CH, p, 192), filtered light falls on a jungle guide in stripes, dressing him in a prisoner's uniform (VR, p. 134)—but even these images imply the metaphysical predicament of men or objects caught in or by some greater power.

The image may portray an attitude: release from the tension of waiting, to reenter the world of action, is expressed as a liberation from prison (LE, pp. 441, 491, 524). A few images relate to gestures: pilots, anxiously waiting for news, pace the floor like prisoners (LE, p. 560), coolies haul loads "with the millenary movement of slaves" (CH, p. 429). Another group qualifies a relationship: one of the few times that Kyo and Tchen experience communion, it is on the basis of a "friendship of prisoners" (CH, p. 288). The relationship may exist between man and object or idea, in which the latter enslaves the former: Tchen enters into terrorist life "as into a prison" (CH, p. 224), Clappique is "chained" to his roulette ball (CH, p. 361), war for soldiers is a prison (NA, p. 257). In a few instances the analogy sets up a physical predicament: men caught in a tank trap feel as though they are in a cell with an inaccessible trapdoor at the top (NA, p. 282); in a few others, a metaphysical predicament, the enslavement of man by a form of destiny. For Kassner, in prison; "the imprisoned stars would revolve about the imprisoned immensity" (TM, p. 60); for Walter Berger, the space between matter and the stars is a prison into which man has been thrown (NA, pp. 98-99).

By far the largest number of images having to do with barriers and prison appear in *La Voie Royale* (over thirty images), in which emphasis on a literal imprisonment is relatively slight (by contrast, there are only about four such images in *Le Temps du mépris* where literal imprisonment is the dominant predicament). In the earlier portion of the novel the images solidify the relationship between Claude and Perken (VR, pp. 31, 53). between Claude and his adventure (VR, p. 55), between Perken and his concept of destiny (VR, p. 84); here a sense of fate is acknowledged, but accepted in principle. The next sequence of images concretizes the challenge: Claude becomes locked in the unrelenting clasp of the stone sculptures (VR, pp. 120, 123, 124) and the forest (VR, pp. 101, 124). The episode that begins with the entry into the area of the savage warriors contains, as we might expect, an abundance of enclosing images, decribing the menace of the jungle (VR, pp. 156,

159), of the savages (VR, pp. 151, 152, 187, 188, 204), Grabot's predicament (VR, pp. 175, 182), the enslavement of Claude and Perken to time (VR, pp. 186, 187). Once Perken has subdued the savages, he no longer feels a prisoner (VR, p. 209); the tables have been turned—now it is the savages who are "imprisoned" by Perken's display of magic (VR, p. 212). From that point on, prison imagery will convey the sense of frustration that precedes Perken's death (VR, pp. 261-62, 262). The prison imagery in this novel, like the animal/insect imagery, thus serves as an important structural rhythm, propelling the story from abstract speculations on destiny, to physical menace, to the final encroachment of destiny itself.

The Military

Military activities play a conspicuous role in all Malraux's novels, and provide a fairly large number of images performing several functions. In *L'Espoir* the military imagery frequently concretizes objects and ideas through animation, personification and even simple allegory. Airplanes have a "threatening patience" and tanks look "astonished" (LE, pp 816, 737). War can advance silently through a city, take on the phantom shape of tanks, and set out bait to catch men (LE, pp. 702, 738, 852). Tanks in particular seem to elicit metaphorical treatment from Malraux: soldiers have a superstitious fear of them, as though they were monsters (CH, p. 204, LE, pp. 628-29), and indeed they are usually depicted as great beasts. Yet they elicit a kind of amusement, too, on Malraux's part, as though their very ungainliness rendered them a bit too fantastic for real warfare.

There are only a few instances of images of the military that sustain important thematic ideas, and they are not recurrent. Claude Vannec, for example, like so many of Malraux's 'conquerors,' is determined to shape his own destiny freely, seeking "his weapons in places where others do not seek theirs" (VR, p. 54). Courage, in *L'Espoir*, is described as something "that must be maintained like rifles" (LE, p. 576). But for the most part military images serve the narrator's need to create certain effects rather than give substance to psychological states or intellectual notions. Analogies to weapons, for example, can create visual resemblances: Clappique carries brooms absurdly like rifles as he gains entry onto a ship (CH, p. 399); firemen futilely aim their hoses at a holocaust as though they were shooting (LE, p. 767); searchlights crisscross the sky, like sabers (CH, p. 231, LE, p. 664). The most frequent recurrences have to do with military advances, assaults, invasions, take-overs, and retreats. These characterize manners of perception of various sorts. Background noises are likened to those of advancing armies: a great confusion of noises and singing, for example, seems "like a marching army approaching" (LE, p. 440); the music in Kassner's vision while he is in prison becomes the "calm of a sunken army" (TM, p. 59). An army on the march, and more generally the image of an assault, give weight and thoroughness to various movements: of fires (VR, p. 258), night (VR, p. 120, TM, p. 56), a plunging plane (LE, p.668), poison gas (NA, p. 205). The image of taking over recurs quite frequently, usually in connection with presences incidental to the main action: the sounds of a violin take over a room (LC, p. 18); similarly, noises (LE, p. 598), heat (VR, p. 224), rain (CH, p. 192), odors (CH, p. 362, LE, p. 621), and anxiety (LC, p. 29) become forces intruding upon the plot. Such elements are thus one of the important groups of devices Malraux employs for "thickening" the atmosphere of the novels.

Notes

1. A recent critic finds three stereotyped roles for women in Malraux's novels: the idealized lady, the suffering mother/wife type (for example, Anna in *Le Temps du mépris*, and the seductive temptress. See Kittye Delle Robbins, "Legends of

Good Women: Medieval Images in the Novels of André Malraux," *Mélanges Malraux Miscellany* 5, no. 2 (Autumn 1973): 3-8.

2. For a fuller discussion of Perken's eroticism, see James C. Nichols, "Malraux's Use of Sexual Metaphor in *La Voie Royale," Mélanges Malraux Miscellany* 6, No. 1 (Spring 1974): 4-14.

3. Joseph Frank, "Malraux's Image of Man," in idem, *The Widening Gyre* (New Brunswick, N.J.: Rutgers University Press, 1963), pp.105-29.

4. For an interpretation of the link between blindness and destiny, see Brian Thompson, "The image of Blindness in Malraux's Meditations on Art," *Mélanges Malraux Miscellany* 3, No. 2 (Autumn 1971): 16-25.

[4]

Imagery of Human Activity

Gambling

What is most striking in Malraux's gambling images is not their number, though that is not inconsiderable (about twenty-eight), nor even particularly their originality, since they are mostly standard commonplaces. It is rather the intense manner in which they characterize, in some of the earlier characters, the overwhelming need to conquer despite unbeatable odds. In *Les Conquérants* Garine thinks of his court trial in Europe as a card upon which he does *not* wish to bet his life; but his youth *is* such a card, and his bet as serious as that of a loser at Monte Carlo who will go off to commit suicide (LC, pp. 45, 48). Later he explains his confidence in the Revolution in the assured tones of the gambler who knows his bet (LC, pp. 140, 143). *La Voie Royale* is replete with figurative gambles describing the individual missions of Claude, for whom the prize may be a gain in virility (VR, pp. 43, 229), of Grabot, for whom gambling represents a means of losing himself in himself (VR, pp. 92, 142), and of Perken (VR, pp. 87, 155). Perken realizes his gamble is enormous; since he *must* bet, he can at least use his twenty tribes as stakes; but at the moment of his death, he is himself his only remaining stake (VR, pp. 87, 90, 264). Obviously Perken will lose his bet. It is equally clear that the mere fact that a character conceives of his life as a bet is a virtual admission that the bet cannot be won, so that the explanation for betting must be sought not in the expectation of a definitive victory but rather in the sheer exaltation of feeling the self pitted so completely against the most formidable opponent of all, death.

Ferral, in *La Condition humaine*, is another inveterate gambler. In his professional work his stakes are the fate of Shanghai; in love, they are his pride (CH, pp. 263, 264, 337, 338, 425). He will of course fail in both. Clappique becomes a gambler through the fatal attraction that a roulette ball, seemingly alive, has over him—and he cedes his will to the ball as though to death itself (CH, pp. 360, 361). Clappique, ironically, will later become a card in Gisors's strategy to save Kyo—this too fails (CH, p. 380). The gambler's obsession seems to have run its course in the later novels.

Art

We have previously seen in a number of instances a recurrent tendency in Malraux to use imagery and atmosphere to create painterly effects. These suggest a familiarity with the techniques of visual composition that is further corroborated in Malraux's use of analogies to the visual arts. These include references to specific painters and paintings, to types of Oriental art and forms, and to types of sculpture. There are, as well, a number of analogies which create simple decorative effects. The lights along the water front of Hong Kong, for example, become a necklace (LC, p. 29), a city sits amidst a harvest like an ornament (LE, p. 554), and lines of dead soldiers lie in garlands (LE, pp. 449, 455).

Images of paintings appear frequently in the novels to set up simple analogies between an experienced reality and the subject matter of a specific painter that comes to the author's mind. The narrator of *Les Noyers de L'Altenburg* recalls his youth at his grandfather's home "with the furtive passage of golden Jews like those of Rembrandt" (NA, p. 43). Guernico is described as "long, pale blond, like so many of Velasquez's portraits" (LE, p. 690). The joy of prisoners is described as not having changed "since Breughel" (NA, p. 28). Similar analogies to genre or period works appear with considerable frequency in *L'Espoir*, where they aid in establishing an epic tone. The distress of peasants fleeing combat is described in terms of a "Flight into Egypt" (LE, p. 627); an outdoor dinner scene becomes an "enormous still life" (LE, p. 604); the backdrop for a peaceful evening is like the "twilight in an equestrian portrait" (LE, p. 505); and militiamen grouped around a cannon are like those in engravings of the French Revolution (LE, p. 464).

Several images relate specifically to Oriental art. In the earlier novels these are usually extensions of real Oriental settings. Rice fields are "large gray mirrors painted here and there, in blurred wash-tints, by bushes and pagodas" (LC, p. 14); Kyo has the "mouth of a Japanese print" (CH, p. 187). Various characters resemble Oriental statuettes; Nicolaieff (LC, p. 155), a Chinese officer (CH, p. 295), a Chinese courtesan (CH, p. 351). But that Malraux's metaphorical interest in Oriental art is abiding is evident in several additional images in the last two novels, all dramatizing a sense of nervous expectation by relating a real nature scene to the fine lines and mists of Japanese prints. A lamp projects the shadow of grass on the face of a wounded man, creating "light, indifferent shadows, painted with a Japanese resolution on these trembling cheeks" (LE, p. 724). A sheet of poison gas passes over trees "letting the sawtooth crests emerge over the backdrop of mist as in Japanese prints" (NA, p. 204). After the gas has passed, all it leaves behind is "the Japanese mist at the bottom of the valley" (NA, p. 209). An apple tree stands out "in a Japanese silhouette against the sky" (LE, p. 827).

What is particularly striking in some of these examples is the close distinctions they elaborate. Clappique evaluates a prostitute as a Rubens, "but not perfect; she must be by Jordaens" (CH, p. 362). Scali, studying Alvear, notices "that the hair modified this Greco as a copy of a baroque painter might have done" (LE, p. 698). This sort of specificity reveals the art connoisseur in certain of Malraux's characters, and there are quite a few of them: not only Clappique, Scali, and Alvear, but Claude Vannec, Gisors, Ferral, Kama, and Vincent Berger as well. But they perhaps also reveal the sheer satisfaction Malraux derives from resorting to a field he knows well. The very number and quality of the art images in the last two novels suggests further that Malraux's sense of visual composition is so well developed, such an integral part of the creative imagination, that it tends to function autonomously, independent of the need to merely illustrate or dramatize. Marcelino, for example, has a face "with the wavy hair of Venetian medallions" (LE, p. 499); Walter Berger has "the broken nose of Michelangelo—a Michelangelo at the end of a long university career. . . . The light shone on his face from below, accentuating the rough-hewn sculptural quality" (NA, pp. 84-85).

Art in these novels is not only expressed through analogical devices, but has become an important theme. In *L'Espoir* it turns up in the conversations of men who can step far enough back from the action to voice a desire to found an artistic style for the Revolution. In a sense Malraux may well be mirroring through allusion to art his own search for a narrative style to support a new kind of novelesque genre that would depict revolution as an ongoing experience. In *Les Noyers de L'Altenburg* allusions center rather on art as content and not style—art as one of the great storehouses of Western culture. While traveling through the wilds of Central Asia, Vincent Berger dreams nostalgically of "inexhaustible museums, covered with paintings up to the ceilings, as in the Dutch paintings that represent the shops of art dealers" (NA, p. 27). But Vincent's later intuitive experiences suggest that what is important in art is not so much the cultural tradition that must be defended in the name of some humanism against such detractors as Möllberg, but rather the spark that seems again and again to be miraculously kindled, as a function of the very tenacity of life, in order to invent the cultural world anew. Whether or not Malraux succeeded in his search in *L'Espoir* may well be a moot point since he never again tried his hand at that sort of fiction. As for his preoccupation with art in the last novel, that was of course to become the central problem that he would study in the long sequence of works on art that mark his subsequent career.[1]

The Strange and Unreal: Ghosts, Dreams, Sleepwalking, Madness, Lunar and Planetary Imagery

Malraux's novels contain such traditional correlatives for situations of unreality as ghosts, dreams, sleepwalking, madness, and lunar and planetary imagery. These images generally express the shock of estrangement from an observed reality. The image of the ghost frequently comes across as a menacing sign of imminent ruin, plunging the observer into a nightmare world. In humiliating Ferral, for example, Valérie has in effect denied the existence of this strong-willed individualist, who now must suffer anguished doubts about his dream of personal dominion over others: "He alone existed in a world of phantoms, and it was *he* who had been flouted" (CH, p. 339). In several instances the image communicates a strange and frightening vision of destruction out of which lone persons or objects loom dramatically into focus to haunt the scene. As Kyo walks into the *Black Cat* nightclub in search of Clappique, the deafening music ceases abruptly and the dancers retreat to their places, with one exception: an aging man, once respectable and now degenerate, who continues to dance alone, attracting the eyes of the other clientele who are roughly in a situation similar to his: "Merchants going into bankruptcy, dancing girls and prostitutes, those who were threatened—almost all of them—kept looking at this ghost, as if he were all alone holding them back at the edge of nothingness" (CH, p. 196).

These signs of destruction carry an obvious ironic impact; men would prefer not to come face to face with the truth of their essential fragility. The ghost image frequently communicates still another kind of irony: a situation is reversed, and an event that had seemed definitive is annulled to permit a counter-action. A Fascist tank in *L'Espoir*, for example, animated as a kind of stupid monster which has not yet understood that the popular forces have secured antitank weaponry, is struck and butts into a rock, "rearing like a ghost of War" (LE, p. 738); this monster-tank has been brought down by an underestimated power, and so the Fascists' illusion of an easy victory is halted. During the bombardment of Madrid, a new wave of fire reaches out to houses already burned: "it lit them from behind, ghostly and funereal, and continued for a long time to prowl behind their lines of ruins" (LE, p. 757); yet underneath the ghostly vision of Madrid's destruction, the journalist Shade will hear the rhythmic voices of invisible people chanting their determination not to give in. When the Germans send out poison gas towards the Russian position, in *Les Noyers de l'Altenburg*, the intervening valley is soon transformed into a mist, "from which emerged alone, absurd and ghostly, a tall telegraph pole" (NA, p. 203). Vincent Berger will undergo a severe shock when he espies a soldier running spasmodically towards him out of the devastation wrought by the gas: "Two yards away the apparition raised its gray face with the white of its eyes gone, and opened its epileptic mouth as if to howl" (NA, p. 231). This phantasm is all that is left of a former human being, a sign of the imminent ruin of Man himself, just as the lone telegraph pole preludes the destruction of the natural world; but the scene will shift from one of phantasmagoric destruction to that of salvation, to become an allegory of man's urgent task to rescue Man from himself.

The image of the aging man on the dance floor, cited above, works in a way that resembles a number of Malraux's analogies to madness. Malraux conceives of the madman as a creature who lives in the closed world of the self, apart from men. He cannot communicate with others, but he has the power to hold the observing eye in a fatal fascination, attracting it to the precarious edge that separates reality from dream, the outer world of action from the prison world of the self.[2] The vertiginous feeling that one is caught in the spell of dreamers or madmen thus appears frequently as a signal that sets going a gnawing questioning of oneself. In *La Condition humaine*, the sense of alienation that weighs upon Kyo as a result of his failure to recognize his own voice on a phonograph record, is painfully aggravated whenever he reflects upon the peculiar madness of his comrade in arms, Tchen. The nature of their relationship baffles Kyo's most intensely sustained hope, which is to break through the barriers of the self in order to establish fraternal bonds. For even when they stand together, as when they join in the attack against the armored train of the enemy, they are none the less worlds apart: "Beneath the brotherhood of arms, at the very moment that he watched this armored train which they would perhaps attack together, he felt the possible split as he might have felt the threat of a fit coming over an epileptic or mad friend at the moment of his greatest lucidity" (CH, p. 274).

Several of the examples in *La Voie Royale* touch on a major theme in that novel—the test of the European mind to rise above the world of dream, and to resist falling into the primitive self symbolized by the jungle and its savages. Claude Vannec detests dreams, and scorns those men for whom adventure is nothing more than "the foodstuff of dreams" (VR, p. 55). Yet he is very much afraid his own scheme to secure lost sculptures from the jungle is mad, until he communicates his plans to Perken: "His plan, as long as he had kept it to himself, had cut him off from the world, had tied him to an incommunicable universe like that of the blind or the mad" (VR, p. 57). The long catalog of descriptions of jungle monstrosities that introduces us to the heart of the adventure culminates with an immense sense of frustration served, fittingly enough, by an analogy to madmen: "What human act here had any sense? What will preserved its power? Everything became dispersed, soft, striving to fit this world that disgusted and hypnotized at the same time, like the stare of an idiot" (VR, pp. 99-100).

The shock communicated by many of the images of dreams and madness thus relates to a menace of a very powerful sort: the possibility of losing one's grip on a determined outer action to fall into the sterility of the self, and all that this entails of a breakdown in effective communication between men. When Vologuine tells Kyo of the official Party attitude towards the revolution in Shanghai, Kyo reacts as a man whose reason for living has suddenly been snatched away from him, and so we read: "Kyo sank lower and lower, as if in a dream" (CH, p. 279). The principal portion of *Le Temps du mépris* depicts the forcible imprisonment of an active man as a near catastrophic fall into the world of dreams and madness. In *L'Espoir*, Magnin is appalled to find his pilots bickering pettily among themselves, and feels as though he were witnessing the worst part of them, "a temporary madness, a dream from which they would sooner or later have to wake up, their crash-helmets over their foreheads, hardened in their flight uniforms, in the reality of death" (LE, p. 683). Vincent Berger, too, has a low opinion of idle dreams, and admits no place for them in his own rather exotic mission in the Orient: "There are few exploits that are nourished rather than rotted by dreams" (NA, p. 64). But that mission will indeed become an idle dream, and he will not understand this until he encounters, in the wilds of Asia, a literal madman who beats him; and so, "broken and unexplainably freed from a spell" (NA, p. 71), he abandons the dream to return to the reality of Europe.

Another important pattern of dreamlike imagery in the novels, to which can be joined a related group of analogies to the lunar and otherworldly, conveys a sense of weirdness to a situation or activity felt as unreal. In some instances the image expresses a reaction to an event almost too much to be hoped for. *Les Conquérants* ends with the gradual crescendo of a distant noise: "It is no longer a hum but a noise composed of successive jolts, quite distant or quite muffled, a dream noise" (LC, p. 161); this turns out to be the long awaited arrival of the Red army. Kassner cannot really believe he is being released from prison: "It was another planet, an unknown world, an arrival in the land of the shades" (TM, p. 116); and outside the prison he finds a "low, gray, dream sky" (TM, p. 119).

In other instances, the image contrasts a strange tranquillity with the frenetic movement of events. Rebecci, for example, has lived through the Chinese revolution "with the serenity of a sleep walker" (LC, p. 23). As Kyo waits to cross over to Hankow to see Vologuine, and receive the news that will crush his hopes, he walks about a neighborhood of small shops: "doctors with toad-signs, dealers in herbs and monsters, public scribes, casters of spells, astrologers, fortune-tellers continued to ply their lunar trades in the dim light into which the blood stains faded" (CH,p. 277). Vologuine will himself strike Kyo as strangely apart from events when he announces his news: "a stiff intensity like that of a sleep walker was all that gave life to this frozen face" (CH, p. 279).

In *L'Espoir* this kind of image applies in a number of instances to planes on bombing missions, relegating them to a realm strangely detached from the frenzied world of fighting. Jaime's plane is just about to fly over the Alcazar when we read: "The circling plane, like a minuscule planet lost in the indifferent gravitation of worlds, waited for Toledo to pass beneath with its rebellious Alcazar and its besiegers, all pulled into the absurd rhythm of terrestial things. . . . It seemed that the whole landscape of clouds was circling around the immobile plane with a planetary slowness" (LE, p. 555). The result of the mission: a successful bombing raid, but the appearance of enemy chasers; and we will learn some pages later that a number of the crew have been killed or wounded, and that Jaime has been blinded (LE, p. 569). After a successful raid over Talavera, Leclerc looks out at the wings of his plane and is startled to find that it has turned a phosphorescent blue; moonlight has transformed the plane into an eerie decor, as though some force beyond man were transmuting the most forceful of actions into a hollow dream: "human gestures were no longer in proportion with things: far from this dial of war, the only illuminated thing for leagues about, the euphoria that follows combat faded into a geological serenity, in the harmony of the moon and this pale metal which shone like stones that shine for thousands of years on dead stars" (LE, p. 618).

At this point it might be interesting to turn back to the passage cited just above, in which Kyo walks among small shops in Hankow, to pick up the next sentence: "The shadows did not so much stretch out to the ground as fade into it, bathed in a blue phosphorescence; the last ray of light of this extraordinary evening that was taking place far away, somewhere among the worlds, bathing the earth with but one reflection, shone weakly in the depth of an enormous arch" (CH, p. 277). The shadows, the ghastly blue phosphorescence, the reference to other worlds prolong the dream image set off by contact with exotic shopkeepers impervious to the outcome of the revolution; and, of course, it turns out that the kaleidoscope of events will render Kyo's revolutionary mission a matter of indifference to all except Kyo and his men. Malraux's dream image, then, has a very strong tendency to turn up a baffling predicament: the man who desires action is warned by dream and madness to keep on a straight course outward from the self, and yet at the very height of what seems successful action the dream image can exert a subtle, but extremely forceful, braking effect by providing a glimpse into the absurdity of action.

Recreation: Circuses, Fairs, Carnivals, Festivals, Sports Events

Another important group of images has to do with circuses, fairs, carnivals, festivals, and sports events—that is, what might together be thought of as a very special sphere of ritualized recreation. At times a visual resemblance between two kinds of activities is sufficient for setting up the analogy. During one of the battle scenes, for example, Tchen looks like a "tight rope walker" as he clambers along a window ledge, followed by the eyes of his men (CH, p. 250). In another battle scene, Siry has not actually seen the Moors attacking, but after the battle the woods are "strewn with Moors like papers after a festivity" (LE, p.715). Fire sparks look like "incandescent confetti" (LE, p. 721) and appear at the end of a fire "as in a well regulated fireworks" (LE, p. 757). The rather large number of these images (about thirty five) in itself suggests a field of experience, presumably one of childhood, that is strongly impressed upon the author's imagination.

These images frequently inject a jarring note of incongruity into serious activity. The appearance and atmosphere of a crowd, in particular, often comes across as some kind of festivity that belies the purpose for its coming together. Kassner, in Prague, visits a political forum called to organize anti-Fascist sentiment, but the forum meets in the "atmosphere of a world championship fight, country fair and threat" (TM, p. 154) and the speeches that ensue will pale before their subject matter: "No human word was as profound as cruelty" (TM, p. 165). For Vincent Berger, the funeral meal that follows his father's death is felt as slightly absurd: "What with the Alsatian *foies gras* following upon the crayfish and trout at this funeral meal, and the raspberry brandy after the Traminer, it would have taken little for the meeting to end up as a country fair'; and he concludes: "The millennia have not been enough for man to learn how to watch people die" (NA, pp. 38-39).

L'Espoir is particularly rich in this kind of image. As they wait for their turn to fly, and perhaps to run out of gas or be shot down, "the volunteers of the international air force, jubilant, their shirts opened in the August heat of Spain, seemed to be coming back from vacation houses and bathing spots" (LE, p. 476). These images are usually associated with contexts of anxious waiting, but their impact, like that of those preceding, is frequently ironic in that they depict a situation that somehow reverses the anticipated one. During the burning of the Alcazar, after the fighting stops abruptly and a polite but cold meeting takes place between the combatants, the observing crowd grows thicker: "their milling about would have taken on the aspect of a Sunday walk if the eyes of all those who were climbing up towards the square had not been stubbornly fixed on the Alcazar" (LE, p. 597). The fierce hostility of the previous hours has suddenly been transformed into an unreal peace. A Fascist officer asks Hernandez to deliver a letter, and Hernandez gallantly agrees. When asked by one of his own officers what this gesture means, Hernandez reflects before answering—and we have another incongruous intrusion: "Knitting his brows, looking more perplexed than ironic, he walked alongside the officer, who was looking at the pavement where the shadow of Mexican hats was casting enormous confetti." And then Hernandez answers: "Generosity" (LE, p.598). Peace seems to have come, but the images insist on an illusion, and Hernandez is taken in by it.

There is another example where the images of a holiday and a circus coincide in the same context. Toledo is threatened by the Fascist army from without and by snipers from within, and the loss of control over the republican soldiers suddenly represents a real danger for Manuel: "the mob was the same as at train stations on major vacation days. . . . Neither the crowd at Toledo up to then, nor that of the Corpus Christi procession of before, nor that of the historic days in Madrid could match this one. The militiamen were holding Mexican hats at the end of their arms, vertically, like circus hoops. Twenty thousand men locked together in madness" (LE, pp. 635-6). Again, the images paint an illusion; in reality, the whole structure of military discipline threatens to crumble before Manuel's eyes. He manages to bring the troops under control, and they are evacuated from the city. Hernandez, with a kind of courage that smacks of proud indifference, prefers to remain with a few men to hold back the enemy invasion of Toledo. The Moors begin their infiltration (it is difficult not to recollect Roland's stand at Roncevaux); and suddenly Hernandez hears a distant noise which his senses question anxiously: "Suddenly, blowing against the direction in which the republicans were running, the wind brought the music of brasses and bass drums, the music of circuses, fairs and armies." This strikes him as absurd; "What merry-go-round was still turning?' Hernandez wondered. He finally recognized the Fascist hymn: the Tercio band was playing on Zocodover Square" (LE, p. 642). Hernandez's heroic stance has been futile; at the very moment he thinks he has held back the enemy, he will be captured by them, and subsequently executed.

Music and Dance

Malraux's use of musical images is fairly extensive, although compared with his art imagery they reveal little knowledge of technique and virtually none of style or history.

Most of the analogies to musical instruments are chosen from the percussion group, and their principal effect, beyond making a good bit of noise, is one of dramatic underscoring. Malraux applies the rhythmic sound of a bell, for example, to convey the throbbing of a wounded knee (VR, p. 240), the anguished beating of a heart (CH, p. 400), the slamming of a tank door (NA, p. 275). The conversation of savages sounds like castanets (VR, p. 205); hail strikes a plane like a tambourine. *L'Espoir* is particularly cacophonous: the noise of a battering ram and of a cannon sounds like a gong (LE, pp. 464, 662); a tray is dropped with the noise of clashing symbols (LE, p. 740); the clocks of Madrid are mixed like piano notes (LE, p. 528). At the end of the novel a feeling of harmony is established when the sounds of running water are figuratively accompanied by a piano (LE, p. 857).

The musical imagery creates other effects as well. An analogy to rising musical scales gives substance to the impression of a sudden, unpleasant start when a character hears frogs croaking in the jungle (VR, p. 86), cart wheels beginning to roll (VR, p. 109), a slamming prison door (TM, p. 90), or a laugh echoed by a passing auto horn (CH, p. 298). In the last two novels the image of leading an orchestra appears several times. In Manuel's case, the branch he constantly needs to hold in his hand becomes symbolic of tentative leadership (LE, pp. 440, 638) until the day comes when his confidence allows him to drop the stick. Walter's hands seem to "'conduct'' the dialogue at the Altenburg (NA, pp. 128, 139); Professor Hoffmann's hand taps out "the funeral march of humanity" as he discusses the use of his poison gas (NA, p. 176).

Malraux gives music a more symbolic connotation in a number of passages. For Kassner, in prison, music becomes a refuge against madness, a form of love that lifts man's head towards manly brotherhood, surmounting everything within him (TM, pp. 52, 53, 59). Yet Kassner will later say that he holds music in horror (TM, p. 180), presumably because of its association with the prison experience. For Gisors, images of music become associated with love, suffering, and death, during his final opiate state (CH, pp. 429, 431), while for Manuel, at the end of *L'Espoir,* music has the power to suppress the will, bringing him relief (LE, p. 857). Music is thus presented as a complex agent of tender, melancholy sensations which gives one relief from anguish, very likely because it is associated with a capacity for human communion—perhaps even love—sensed at an instinctive, interior level rather than projected through the will and exterior action.

Malraux's use of song images supports this view; they can depict suffering, but they tend to be framed in universal or even epic proportions. Men work together in exhilaration, and their song becomes the outward projection of their latent nobility as they fight, even through death, against their low condition. The fate that Kyo has accepted, for example, envelops him "with the majesty of a funeral song" (CH, p. 406). A triumphant crowd of republicans in *L'Espoir* shouting greetings seems "united by this cry as though by a constant and brotherly chorus" (LE, p. 469). Literal singing is particularly frequent in *L'Espoir* (see, for example, LE, pp. 441, 461, 474, 632). At one point Moreno describes the feeling of a man fighting, knowing he will surely die: "you possess what is best in everyone. You possess their . . . well, their best part, like the joy of a carnival crowd. . . . I have a pal who calls that the moment when the dead start singing" (LE, p. 743). When Madrid is being shelled, the American newspaperman, Shade, hears a distant noise that sounds like the beating of funeral drums; it will turn out to be the noise of a "human drum," the people of Madrid rhythmically shouting: "no pasarán"—they shall not pass (LE, p. 757).

A few of Malraux's music images, and virtually all of his dance images, create an effect of incongruity by directing the imagination to the spectacular or fantastic. In *L'Espoir* the image of performing musicians appears several times to set up a sense of unreality in an observing character who cannot quite fathom the significance of the scene he is witnessing. After his plane crashes on a coastal Spanish road, Attignies, still suffereng from his wounds and in a state of semi-shock, sets out to find aid for his men amidst the confusion of an enormous crowd fleeing a Fascist advance. He looks up at the road: "Above the embankment, busts were bent over towards the west, walking and running. In front of a number of mouths a fist held a vague object, as if they were all playing on silent bugles: they were eating. A short, wide vegetable, celery perhaps" (LE, pp. 794-95). The series of hallucinatory visions will continue until he reaches a telephone station, only to find that the lines have been cut. The image of violinists playing their instruments applies, in two or three instances, to wounded men wearing plaster casts on their arms; the picture is slightly grotesque, and the effect is that of suggesting a bitter irony. When Manuel, for example, begins singing the *Tantum Ergo* in homage to Guernico, the men about join in the chorus: "Just as his friends had rediscovered this lightly ironical Latin, the wounded rebels, with their arms bent in plaster casts upon which they seemed to be getting ready to play violins, rediscovered the Latin of death" (LE, p. 697).

The image of a strange dance works in a similar manner: Malraux transforms the movements of men in a grim context into a surrealistic dream ballet. Fascist planes begin bombing a military hospital, and Ramos organizes the evacuation of the soldier inmates: "Other wounded men, with their arms in casts, slid by as though in a lugubrious ballet, at first black in profile, then their light-colored pajamas becoming redder and redder as they crossed the square in the somber glow of the fire" (LE, p. 722).[5] After poison gas has been propelled in the direction of the Russian trenches, in *Les Noyers de l'Altenburg,* the German troops move out to cross through the barbed wire fence protecting the Russian position. Vincent's binoculars frame the scene dramatically for us:

> "Human spots began to become entangled in the network of barbed wire, jigging about like spiders on an invisible web, for my father could only see the poles. After the persistent movement forward which the distance slowed down as it had slowed down that of the gas, there followed a long Punch and Judy show on the spot, a sinister dance which did not end. Finally, they all plunged into the Russian trench." (NA, p. 213)

This long, suspenseful dance is "sinister" because it should be the one that culminates in the destruction of the Russians by the Germans. But Vincent has been hasty; he suddenly modifies his statement, in preface to the modification of the entire scene: "No, a few were stopping at the barbed wire." We do not need to be told why—the soldiers have been taken aback by something horrendous they have seen. Instead of advancing the soldiers will retreat; instead of killing the Russians, the Germans will attempt to rescue them.

Literature, the Theater, the Cinema

Malraux's ironic transpositions from the realm of the real to that of the arts are most often grounded in allusions to the literary, the theatrical, and the cinematic. The effect, when applied to a character, is frequently that of comic grotesqueness. Rebecci, the Genoese "sleepwalker," is a believer in demons and magic, a daydreamer whose visions turn most often to finer versions of the same cheap stuff he sells: mechanical toys and souvenir junk. Physically, he is a comic figure: "often, at siesta time, one could see his white shape wandering about: his flat cap, narrow body, enormous pants that bicycle clips transformed into the pants of a Zouave, and his Chaplinesque feet sticking out" (LC, p. 24).

He has the head of a Punch figure; Garine had named him "Gnafron" (LC, p. 27).

Rebecci is a rather sketchy character; his counterpart in *La Condition humaine* is a masterfully drawn creature of dreams. Clappique is the very incarnation of incongruity: a moonstruck teller of extravagant tales, a "Pulchinello" disguised in a tuxedo, a "Fantomas" who will look into a mirror to see himself transformed into a "gargoyle" and a "carnival samurai." This sham buffoon, strangely, keeps turning up in some of the most important contexts of action, as though to contaminate with his own unreality the possibility of a real victory. Just as Malraux's incongruous image generally provokes a feeling of anxiety within the subjectivity of a character, the appearance of this incongruous figure intrudes an element of anxiety upon the movement of action and plot. Like the odd side of a coin, Malraux has made him inseparable from the face side of action, in the same way that he has characterized Rebecci as the "midwife" for the terrorist Hong. Where the genuine heroes exteriorize myth Rebecci and Clappique interiorize it, and the mere fact of their presence becomes a mocking sign exposing the element of madness and dream lying beneath the lucidity that leads to action.

Comic effects seem normal enough in the case of these two bizarre creatures; but they communicate a sense of incongruity in some of the characterizations of serious men, as well. Katow's extreme experiences in Russia, for example, have stamped his face with an expression of ironic naiveté. As Tchen addresses him, in a room dramatically framed by an overhead light, he sees "this nice Russian Pierrot face—small laughing eyes and a stubbed nose—that even this light could not make dramatic"; but the narrating voice, as though to strip off the mask of irony momentarily to presage the final, consummately dramatic role that will be Katow's, reports through Tchen's mind: "he, however, knew what death was" (CH, p. 188).

In *L'Espoir*, Scali, "with his round glasses, his overly-long trousers with billowing legs, his look of an American comic star in an aviation film" (LE, p. 672), is not really a comic figure, but as an art historian and intellectual he does seem somewhat out of place in a wartime atmosphere; and indeed, he is one of the principal figures in the novel whose participation questions the meaning of war. Möllberg, in *Les Noyers de l'Altenburg*, is bald and thin and has pointed ears, so that he reminds Vincent of "vampires in children's tales" (NA, p. 107); he also looks like the statuette "monsters" of his own making that represent fantastic, semihuman creatures (NA, pp. 108, 129). Why Malraux should insist on this manner of resemblance several times is of some importance. This intellectual who has peered into the dark recesses of time and culture, who has brought back his gloomy analysis of the meaning of Man, has also lost sight of men themselves. He fashions grotesque figures and, ironically, looks like them himself, because like Goya's sad monsters he only has a dim memory of once having been human. All of these ironies, then, express paradoxes. Katow's naive look seems to conceal a great depth of hard experiences, and yet those experiences have prepared him to face life, and death, with greater simplicity. Scali's comic look seems to conceal a serious intellectual who has voluntarily involved himself in a war, but the reasons for war may sometimes baffle the intellectual. Möllberg's comically grotesque look seems to conceal a brilliant mind that has searched for an answer to the enigma of Man, but the enigma has only mocked him by proposing an answer which he accepts as *the* answer, and to which he has himself conformed.

Characterizations such as those of Katow and Scali have comic elements; but Rebecci and Clappique, as we have seen, are not only comic but fantastic, and they are not the only such figures in the novels. Towards the end of *L'Espoir*, just before the image of an Indian decor done in *trompe-l'oeil* will insist, once again, that peace and victory are but an illusion (LE, pp. 856-57), an eccentric old man will suddenly appear from nowhere. Formerly with a circus in India, knowledgeable in antiquities, "with the face and gestures of born actors, of those who can only live in fiction" (LE, p. 850), he has a number of familiar characteristics; and he will let us know that wars may come and wars may go, but the principal enemy of man is an inhuman force that would undo, in short order, the works of civilization if man were to let up in his efforts against that force. His particular form of "lunar" trade: he is a museum guide.

But there is another character, too, who shares more than one trait in common with Rebecci and Clappique, and that is Möllberg. Where the former is a dealer in art junk and the latter in art objects, Möllberg is a scholar in human artifacts—but also a fashioner of figurines. All three have had the dizzying experience of falling into the bottomless well of a distant culture—the first two in Asia, Möllberg in Africa. All three are "lunatic"—Rebecci plies a "lunar" trade, Clappique claims he will die "while going to pick the moon out of a pond" (CH, p. 197), and Möllberg's scholarly findings center about the fascination of primitive peoples with the moon. All have had visions of dreams and monsters, and in a very real sense have looked into the mirror of reality to see themselves reflected as grotesque creatures. And in all three, the lines of direct action and the unreality of dream, fiction, and art seem to converge as though to prove definitively that those lines are never strictly parallel (although Kassner's experience in his prison cell leaves little to doubt here, in any case). The principal difference in these characters is that the former two come across as unsubstantial spirits whose presence has an insidious effect upon action, whereas in Möllberg the author has spelled out terms objective enough for the hero to grapple with directly (the idea of "grappling" may perhaps recall the sequence to which Malraux's last novel was to belong: "La Lutte avec l'Ange," "The Struggle with the Angel").

Another pattern of imagery of the arts functions in a manner similar to one which we have by now seen several times: a figure intrudes incongruously to suggest an ironic situation. Tcheng-Dai's death in *Les Conquérants* is immediately seized upon by Garine as a chance to rally prorevolutionary sentiment among the people. We know the English did not kill him, but the funeral does indeed turn into political propaganda, and the theatrical image suggests a sham decor; the narrator reports: " 'Death to the English brigands,' I manage to read just as the strange symbol disappears, hidden by the corner of the street as by a theater prop" (LC, p. 128). In an early, wildly undisciplined battle of *L'Espoir*, the anarchist Puig sends cars to crash through a military barricade and seize a cannon emplacement: "In a howling of honks and horns, two Cadillacs came up zigzagging wildly as in gangster films" (LE, p. 453). The drivers succeed, but die in the process; the reaction of the Negus: "It's a respectable job, but not a serious job" (LE, p. 453). None the less, Puig tries the same tactic himself on another cannon position: "Puig could see the gunners who were no longer protected by their bullet-shield zoom larger as in the movies. A Fascist machine gun kept shooting and zooming larger" (LE, p. 454).

Allusions to the cinema can no doubt be accounted for, in part, by Malraux's strong interest in film techniques. In *L'Espoir* they also aid in establishing an aesthetic distance between reader and action, in such a way as to transpose chaotic activity into controlled, epic spectacle. During the bombing of Madrid, for example: "A building was burning as in the movies, from top to bottom" (LE, p. 746); a portion of the battle for the Manzanares is witnessed for us by the novice soldier Siry, who at one point reports: "Nation after nation, companies go by, in the mist which now seems like the smoke of explosions, bent forward, rifles ahead. Like in the movies, and yet so different! Each of these men is one of his own" (LE, p. 716). But it is very often the case that

Malraux's cinema images take on the same connotations as those of the theater, and these usually suggest an ironic hollowness beneath supposedly solid activity. The message comes through quite clearly in a number of clichés of the "comic opera" type. Garine wishes to make an efficient weapon out of his "comic opera office" (LC, p. 52), and will later recall his successful mission in China: "To think that when I came here, in Lambert's time, Canton was a republic out of comedy!" (LC, p. 160). In *L'Espoir* the Spanish army suffers from a reputation of being an "operetta" army, and it is Manuel's goal to remold it into a serious enterprise: "There are no operetta armies, Ramos my friend, there are only operettas about the army. What they call an operetta army is an army of civil war" (LE, p. 506).

The meaning suggested by such images can be extended to cover more subtle situations, where the conditions of action itself are put into question by the ironic intrusion. Examples abound in *L'Espoir*. The opening days of the war in Spain come across as a beautiful spectacle of fraternal action, but that action, as the Negus informs Puig in the passage cited above, is simply not serious—the fighters have not learned the true cost of action. During a heated battle, for example: "Carrying their rifles, fellows would bring over the news just as, in studio bars, actors come and drink in their costumes, between two film shots"; but by contrast: "on the white stones of the checkerboard flagging of the bar, were bloodied sole-prints" (LE, p. 464). The arms seized by the popular forces, in one romantic episode, include a jumble of modern rifles and "theater sabres" (LE, p. 467). At one point during the early joyous days of victory, in Madrid, Lopez shouts facetiously: " 'On stage there,' he bellowed: 'they're about to start shooting the film!' In the full light of the flash lights, Madrid, costumed in all the disguises of the revolution, was an immense nocturnal studio" (LE, p. 468). Once the anti-Fascist forces become better organized, a more careful screening of prospective volunteers ensues: "the brigades were formed of fighters, not movie extras" (LE, p. 665).

Garcia will explain Hernandez's gallant action in Toledo in these terms: "You know very well that there is quite a bit of theater at the beginning of any revolution; at this moment, here, Spain is a Mexican colony. . . ." (LE, p. 607). There are indeed a number of allusions to things Mexican in *L'Espoir*: literal Mexican soldiers who look like Pancho Villa and such patently unreal decor as the sombreros cited earlier in connection with Hernandez's romantic gesture and Manuel's evacuation of his troops. One may or may not question the desirability of Lopez's dream of a new revolutionary style born of the war in Spain, as was the case in Mexico (cf. LE, p. 472); but one must question—and the images aid us in doing so—whether one can win a difficult war in a play atmosphere.

Domestic Life

The final group of images to be considered here are those drawn from domestic life. These include a wide variety of analogies having to do with traveling, games and toys, sports, school experiences, professions and trades, as well as various other sources that do no recur with any great frequency but which together belong to the realm of ordinary, or even trivial, experience and activity. Many of them set up simple visual resemblances: jungle temples are built like "domino castles" (VR, p. 49), Vincent Berger has the fine hands of a fencer (NA, p. 48), and various characters look like boxers, wrestlers, peasants, businessmen, carpenters, and so forth. Others characterize motions, manners, or attitudes. A violent movement is described by analogy with rolling balls (CH, p. 254); a plane's noise is like that of a race car (LE, p. 717); men are packed as tightly as matches (LE, p. 442). Garine has the energy of a peasant (LC, p. 54),

Leclerc has their ruse (LE, p. 672), Claude's grandfather takes pride in his ships the way peasants do when they fondle their animals (VR, p. 26). Several characters raise a professorial index finger or take on a professorial tone, perhaps as a function of Malraux's own ironic self-awareness of the highly intellectual nature of quite a bit of the dialogue (LE, pp. 551, 603, 646, 702, NA, p. 196).

But many of the images of domestic life belong to a pattern of some significance by virtue of a traditional poetic function: by relating to what is by nature commonplace they can inject an ironic note of casualness into what otherwise seems quite serious. One of the effects Malraux achieves through them is an abrupt sense of finality. Katow, for example, awaiting death in the prison yard, wonders why the atmosphere seems nocturnal despite the presence of light: " 'Is it because of the wounds,' Katow wondered, 'or because we are all lying down, as in a station?' " The image of the train station then suddenly transforms his questioning into a certitude of the future: "This *is* a station. We will go off for nowhere, and that's it. . . ." (CH, p. 400). Just before he is led off to a death by torture, he consoles himself by reflecting: "Come on! Let's just suppose I died in a fire" (CH, p. 411). The image here underscores a self-conscious, ironic heroism, but it is also of a general sort that recurs frequently in the novels, and the sense is usually the same: a tragic or spectacular way of dying is really like the most ordinary way—what is certain is the irreversible movement towards death itself. Möllberg employs a medical figure in a similar manner to strikingly dramatic effect when he describes the fatalism of primitive societies who would murder their rulers according to the movement of the heavenly bodies. The rulers understood perfectly well that they must die: "They were no more ignorant of it than a doctor with uremia or cancer is ignorant of the final outcome of uremia and cancer: tied to heaven as we are to our microbes. Almost all the dignitaries followed them into death. They would die of the King's death just as we die of a blood clot" (NA, p. 132).

Among the more interesting examples of domestic images are those in which a wry sense of humor works its way into an essentially grim context. Kyo visits his military posts: " 'I'm becoming the milkman making his rounds,'—thought Kyo" (CH, p. 234). The insurgents' battle planes are in a bad state: "Henceforth, the enemy was less the Fascist army than it was the motors of these old planes, covered with patches like old pants" (LE, p. 615). The following passage contains, in addition to the cliché of a sieve and the surprise effect of a wash hanging up to dry, a good example of some of the strange art effects Malraux enjoys elaborating in *L'Espoir*, and the extra bit of jovial humor that comes from intimacy with statues in the section of the novel recounting the battle of Toledo:

> The militiamen kept shooting, in a boiler room atmosphere, their naked torsos speckled with spots of light like panthers speckled with black spots: the enemy shells had made a sieve of the upper part of the brick wall. Behind Garcia, on the outstretched arm of an apostle, machine gun belts were drying like a wash. He hung his leather jacket on its extended finger. (LE, p. 539)

In such cases as these the images do not so much express an anxiety as exorcise it, reducing the mortal menace of combat to a human, comprehensible level. To this extent they may also be thought of as confirmations of innocence. Malraux's sentimental bias in favor of man, as we have previously seen in connection with the child image, comes through on a number of occasions, recalling to his reader the essential simplicity and vulnerability of man, as opposed to the complex, hostile reality he must confront. Images of domestic life, and especially those in which a childlike quality in man is made manifest, often underscore this attitude. When Tchen, for example, looks over the weapons possessed by his group of men, he notices that one of them has nothing better than nails which he apparently plans to strew on the street to wound the hooves of horses: "A teenager was looking over big wide-headed nails, like seed, which he pulled out of his bag" (CH, p. 244). The image colors the activity with a heavy bias in favor of the insurgents, who must temporarily forgo the innocent, almost touching, acts of ordinary life to take up arms against their oppressors.

Confrontations: Patterns of Irony

Many of the images having to do with human activities, as we have seen, create an ironic effect because of an element of incongruity. These images constitute one of the most striking patterns in Malraux's work, at an expressive as well as functional level, and deserve closer consideration. The kinds of images involved are drawn from fairly wide and varied areas of experience and phenomena. But a second glance will suggest that a unitive thread runs through a goodly number of them. Some have to do with the mysterious realm beyond man's conscious life, others with spectacle and the arts, still others with the ordinary circumstances of life and its normally innocent aspects. Together, they relate to what might be thought of as "pseudo" experiences—those of relatively insignificant importance, or else those wherein action is executed in a fantasy realm remote from man's genuine impositions upon reality. As such, they tend to function as shadow images for his important acts. If one may conceive of direct confrontation as a kind of exploration of man's relationship to the universe, the shadow image then represents a mirroring of that confrontation in another, muted register. For the split second of anxious shock, it estranges the character from the context of the real action in which he seems very solidly engaged, and calls into question the anterior assessment of his relationship to the world.

Several patterns of confrontation are regularly served by the images that intrude an element of incongruity. A particularly significant one is the confrontation with death. In one of the analogies to domestic life the absurdity latent in incongruity comes to the surface and effectively dramatizes a profound sense of physical disgust and psychological dismay. This is the event that leads Garine to abandon the army in Europe: "Up to then, the legionnaires had at certain times received short daggers, which still seemed to be war weapons; on that day they received new knives, with brown wooden handles and a wide blade, resembling—in a disgusting and terrible way—kitchen knives" (LC, p. 47). Kitchen knives, in their usual context of a domestic sphere, are inoffensive objects. But the simile sets up a clash that releases the mind from its habitual mode of thinking, to precipitate a new insight. One level of meaning might be this: a man may not find anything shocking about killing with a bayonet, but he is not normally prepared to kill with a kitchen knife; so that the domestic intrudes to accuse the military, to expose it, and thereby correct Garine's previous blindness to a truth lying beneath a ritual mask: the end of fighting is murder.

Another, more subjective, meaning might also be read in Garine's shock: the discovery in himself, through the recollection of a familiar object, of one extreme and perverse form of potential human contact—the penetration of flesh. This reading might be further substantiated by reference to the one prolonged episode in Malraux's novels where a man consummates just such a contact: Tchen's murder of his sleeping victim. In this case Tchen stands before his victim holding a razor in his right hand, a dagger in the left: "The razor was surer, but Tchen felt he could never use it; the dagger repulsed him less" (CH, p. 182). This impending contact between one man and another is further rendered grotesque for us by an analogy to the inoffensive contact of dancing: "Thus he held the dagger with its blade up, but the left side of the man's chest was further away from him: through the mosquito netting he would have to strike at full arm's length with a curving motion like that of swing" (CH, p. 182-82).

Point-blank murder does not come easily for Malraux's man. In *L'Espoir*, the Negus is deeply impressed with the fact that a Fascist officer, with ample opportunity to aim his flamethrower against the Negus before being fired upon himself, does not do so. The episode in question comes across as a richly staged dream spectacle, with a setting that includes underground corridors, blue phosphorescent lighting, and a dance of maddened shadows projected upon the walls. The Negus shoots; the Fascist "finally slid alongside the Negus, with the slow motion of movies, his head in the jet of flames" (LE, p. 544). And it seems likely that Malraux has transformed this battle into the kind of unreal spectacle it is precisely to focus upon the disquieting lesson that the Negus will learn: "you just can't use the thrower against somebody looking at you. You don't dare . . . You really don't dare . . . ." (LE, p. 545). Are we to understand this as a kind of tribute being paid to the enemy? It is more to the point to think of it as a discovery of human qualities in the enemy—no matter which side a man may choose on the political spectrum, he still remains essentially a man.

The Fascist's act illustrates a dilemma. Where action must culminate in murder, it is disastrous to hesitate—hesitations leave one open to an invasion of doubts that can only corrode action, and besides they give the adversary time to be the first to kill. But on the other hand, that very moment of hesitation is itself revelatory of an instinctively held value: human life. To veil that instinct seems to be one of the heaviest prices one must pay for acting effectively. Garine, in the passage cited above, encounters his fascination and balks at it; he is still profoundly vulnerable. Later in the novel he will have to kill one enemy agent in order to terrify another into revealing important information. Then he will not hesitate; he has learned his lesson all too well. Tchen must encounter his fascination at the very beginning of the action in which he is to play a role; he too hesitates momentarily, but, fatally, succumbs to go on to become a dehumanized agent in the service of death.

The union of human beings through killing, like all other confrontations, can of course be viewed from two opposing sides. It is natural enough to expect a reaction of terror when the predicament is that of suddenly becoming aware that one is going to be killed. In these instances, too, we find Malraux resorting to incongruous imagery to express a sense of the grotesque. "They were in here as if inside a shooting booth at the fair" (VR, p. 180)—this is what comes to Claude Vannec's mind as he realizes his group, badly protected by their flimsy hut, are completely surrounded by savages who show every sign of wanting to do them in by shooting arrows. A more subtle instance occurs in the scene of Hernandez's execution where Malraux works out an entire process of coming to awareness through shock. The execution is represented in Hernandez's mind as a ritual to be eternally repeated: "At this hour, on half of the land of Spain, adolescents caught in the same hideous comedy are shooting into the same dazzling mornings and the same peasants, with the same hair combed forward, are falling or jumping into ditches " (LE, p. 651). Since it is a Spaniard who reflects for us, the ritual is conceived of in terms of a traditional Spanish heroism, with allusions to such virtues as "nobility of character," "courage," and "generosity"; yet, given the immediate context of the firing squad, the virtues seem totally out of place, and the images that come to Hernandez's mind transform the event into a horrible parody of life. His reaction to the bodies being shot into the ditch: "Only at the circus had Hernandez ever seen a man jump backward" (LE, p. 651). The vanquished, incredibly, seem to want to cooperate with the victors in this strange ritual:

> One of them doesn't know if he is supposed to stand with his face or back forward. "People never know what position to take when the train leaves," Hernandez thinks hysterically. . . . And the prisoners seem to be helping them—trying to understand what is wanted of them, to conform to it. "You'd think they were going to a funeral."

And Hernandez adds with a certitude now beyond despair: " 'They are going to their own.' . . . 'Are they going to stop soon arranging these prisoners as though for a marriage photograph, in front of these horizontal rifle cannons?' . . . Hernandez thinks of Pradas, of generosity. The three prisoners are finally facing forward: The photograph is definitely ready." And now he understands, too late to rescue himself from the effects of the sense of fatalism that led him to be captured in the first place and, more profoundly, from the theatrical gallantry that he had tried to assimilate to war: "Generosity is being the winner" (LE, pp. 651-52).

There is another pattern of confrontation in which the incongruous image dramatizes a powerful shock of estrangement: the spectacle of the defeat of man. We are dealing here with one of the obsessive themes in Malraux, perhaps nowhere more concisely summarized than in *Les Noyers de l'Altenburg,* where the narrator recalls Pascal's well known image: "Let one imagine a great number of men in chains, all condemned to die, of whom some being each day slaughtered in the sight of the others, those who remain see their own condition in that of their fellow men . . . . That is the image of the human condition" (NA, p. 289). This painful reality—and it is an everpresent one—consistently offers the mind more than it can cope with, and drives it anxiously into the deep recesses of an unreal nightmare world. Such signs of ruin as the ghost image considered earlier are but one particularly recurrent, hence more visible, means of communicating shock, but their sense carries over as a general formulaic pattern to numerous episodes.

In the earlier novels, these episodes tend to be structured in pairs, in such a way that character "x," who witnesses ruin in character "y," will himself become a ruin to be witnessed by character "z," thus guaranteeing the effectiveness of the estranging ghost formula: the foreboding will eventually be realized in fact, underscoring its general applicability to everyone. Garine, for example, witnesses Klein's mutilated cadaver; later the narrator will witness the decline of Garine. Perken will find in Grabot a "powerful ruin," but at the end of the novel Claude Vannec will witness the ruin of Perken; in the first case, the very specific correlative for estrangement and futility is blindness, in the second the loss of feeling in Perken's hand. When, in *La Condition humaine*, May tells of her infidelity to Kyo, his reaction is as follows: "he seemed to be watching May die like this, watching the form of his happiness disappear absurdly, like a cloud being absorbed into the grey sky" (CH, p. 214). Malraux will later repeat the image of disappearing clouds when he has Gisors reflect over Kyo's death: "Clouds were passing over the dark pines and were gradually being absorbed into the sky; and he thought that one of their groups, that one specifically, expressed the men he had known or loved, and who were dead" (CH, p. 431). From *La Condition humaine* on, the principal characters tend to survive their predicaments, and the ghost formula of shock applies more broadly to men in general rather than to specified individuals.

Of these spectacles of man's defeat, Malraux's hospital scenes are particularly well served by images that depict an anxious dream reality. In *Les Conquérants*, Garine's developing illness necessitates a trip to the hospital, where the narrator visits him. The narrator's description of the scene contains elements that affect the meaning in both obvious and subtle ways. Garine is shown to be in bed, lying behind half-raised tulle curtains. As the narrator, tired and perspiring, tries to relax, his senses begin to perceive a number of signals outside: mosquitoes buzzing, the mixed odors of decomposition, of sweet flowers, stagnant water, tar, and iron. He hears distant Chinese cries, horns, and firecrackers. The isolated strains of a one-stringed violin leads him to conjecture a wandering show or else some artisan playing, half dozing, in his boarded up shop. Finally, the visual effects of the distant light and smoke of the city remind him of some vast country fair (LC p. 113).

The decor in this passage plays its usual important role in determining the total effect. There are, as is often the case in Malraux's scenes of foreboding, "the eternal mosquitoes." There is the same sort of dramatic separation from the world that we find at the beginning of *La Condition humaine*, creating the effect of a sacred place. There is even the same mosquito netting, a veiled sanctuary to which a man might come to probe a mystery. In the "sanctuary" hut of *La Voie Royale* Perken's probe of Grabot will elicit a one-word response: "Nothing"; Tchen's probe will end with an act of murder; here the accumulation of significant detail suffices to convey what the probe is about and what the answer is, without the need for explicit comment. The hypersensitive narrating voice registers for us the odors of decomposition and stagnation, and the sounds of noises. Then the noises become music, leading us to imagine either the presence of a nearby theater or the kind of artisan who is usually depicted elsewhere as plying a "lunar" trade, and the passage concludes with the analogy to a fair—precisely the phenomena of that kind of shadow activity Malraux employs to expose the underside of serious action. The entire scene thus projects, in a coolly controlled manner, the anxiety of the narrator and a general sense of the vanity of action in the face of Garine's symbolic defeat.

In one particularly lengthy hospital episode, in *L'Espoir*, the incongruous images take over the development of a troubling theme. Manuel is just beginning to understand what war is: "to do the impossible in order for pieces of iron to penetrate living flesh" (LE 509). On his way to Barca's hospital room he must pass through an enormous ward with a high ceiling: "and these people in pajamas, whose rickety bodies slipped by on crutches in the uneasy peace of the hospital, these shadows dressed in bandages like mid-Lent costumes, all this seemed an eternal realm of wounds, founded there outside of time and the world." He is relieved to be able to leave this "aquarium" to go through a normal hospital room, "so different from the Inquisition Chamber where the bandaged ghosts slid by." When he arrives in Barca's room the conversation soon turns to the question of what prompts ordinary men to take sides, knowing the price that must be paid—and the images intrude again: "In the aquarium, men on crutches were slipping through the frame of the open door, one behind the other." Leaving Barca, Manuel must pass through the way he entered; and the spectacle of men who have become vestiges of action, question marks at the end of a heroic affirmation for justice, now explodes into a massive display of surrealistic transformations before Manuel's bewildered eyes:

> Through the open door of the great ward, with their profiles of footsore soldiers of the Great Companies, the wounded with plaster arm casts passed, their arms, sausaged with cloth, held far from their bodies by the strap, like violinists holding their violin up against their necks. Those were the most disturbing of all: a plaster-cast arm looks like a gesture, and all these ghostly violinists, holding out their immobilized, rounded arms, advanced like statues that were pushed, in the aquarium silence reinforced by the hidden buzzing of flies. (LE, p. 514)

Ironic figures dramatize still another kind of confrontation, a spectacle in which man's questioning of other men is carried to the extreme limits of an Inquisition. All of the novels contain at least one interrogation scene in which a character is forcibly obliged to give an account of himself to another, and all but one such scene is given an absurd cast through reference to incongruous imagery. The exception occurs in *La Voie Royale*, where the dialogue between Claude Vannec and the director of the French Institute informs us explicitly of Claude's sense of frustration. This is the one novel in which the inquisitioner is the nonhuman universe; in all the others it is man himself. In *Les Conquérants* the scene has to do with a parody of conventional legal justice. Garine, brought to court for his aid in an abortion case, must stand trial: "During the whole length of the trial, he had the impression of an unreal spectacle; not of a dream, but of a strange comedy, rather vile and completely lunar. Only the theater can give an impression of convention as strongly as a court inquest" (LC, p. 45). This experience will both expose him to the intense humiliation Malraux associates with imprisonment and initiate in him the misanthropy that will endure, paradoxically, at the very moment he is heading a revolution ostensibly in the name of the people.

During König's interrogation of Kyo, the latter accepts the offer of a slice of bread: "Kyo remained standing (there was no seat) in front of the desk, biting into his bread like a child. After the abjectness of prison, everything had taken on an unreal lightness for him" (CH, p. 393). König begins his bluff: he stages a series of telephone rings which are supposed to induce Kyo into revealing information. Kyo finally understands the trick: "He thought that the telephone call was an even worse staging" (CH, p. 394). The fundamental characteristics of this sort of scene, then, are a focus on innocence, the fall into a dreamlike state, and a cheap theatrical staging on the part of inquisitioners who none the less take themselves very seriously. But it is no less interesting to note that the questioning *does* oblige the character to formulate an answer, satisfactory both to himself and to the adversary, as to why he is involved in his action. Given the extreme difficulty of the task—the accused character may have to lie to appease his judges, and in any case may not be entirely sure he can reconcile idea and action even for himself—the event comes across as a particularly painful experience in which a sense of futility is joined to that of humiliation.

Le Temps du mépris opens with an interrogation scene staged by Nazi inquisitioners. As Kassner awaits his turn he must witness the humiliating grilling of another Communist captive: "Kassner imagined himself in the place of the communist, at the same time a distressed spectator and actor, and began to lose lucidity" (TM, p. 21). The notion that he must himself conceal his identity, forced to play an odious role wherein he must become "inauthentic" in order to save his skin, fills him with intense uneasiness. Malraux even has Kassner go through the patently melodramatic act of swallowing a secret paper—and Kassner recalls with a heightened sense of the grotesque "the cardboard odor of carnival masks" (TM, p. 26).

A similarly painful spectacle occurs in *Les Noyers de l'Altenburg*, where Vincent Berger is called in to record the interrogation of a captured Russian woman suspected of spying. There is a particularly well developed sense of the incongruous here. Again, images of innocent domesticity intrude to intimate the absurd: "They had stripped her of her clothes to search her and had given her a black blouse like a schoolgirl smock" (NA, p. 161); "She watched him with an uneasy intenseness: she was a giant with a snub nose and small bright eyes, a rather nice Pinocchio face. Still rubbing her hands against her black smock with the gesture of a cook before her masters" (NA, p. 163). She plays her womanly powers of seduction against the interrogator, Captain Wurtz; he informs her that she may very well be shot, and her shocked reaction ("Women aren't shot!") reminds us of the effect of a domestic image cited earlier: one might accept the execution of men, but not of women. The determining factor for making her talk is the introduction into the room of a young boy—and the narrator reflects: "Why in the devil had he always thought that women spies don't have children?" (NA, pp. 164-65). The whole scene is, of course, a staged affair, and there are the usual allusions to the theatrical: "Her 'for goodness' sake' had something theatrical about it, which was marked even more by her Russian accent. Besides, everyone was playing a role" (NA, p. 162). The woman senses the presence of the boy: "as though this noise had touched, not the character she was trying to play, but the terrified character she was hiding, she suddenly turned around" (NA, p. 165).

Vincent reacts with an overwhelming sense of shock and shame: "He felt he would not be able to take notes" (NA, p. 165); "My father did not know that it was possible for him to suffer from shame to that extent. His muscles tightened, just as when someone hears a shell coming" (NA, p. 166). The end result: the woman will be executed, and Vincent will ask for, and receive, permission to leave the secret service. But not before he receives a lesson from Wurtz: " 'Acts such as these, of which you are afraid,' the captain had said, 'save the lives of thousands of our soldiers' " (NA, p. 167). Vincent reflects that his previous action had been of a political nature, "not of a policeman," and thereby voices one of the recurring stumbling blocks we find in Malraux, the unresolved dilemma of the intellectual and moralist reflecting upon the nature of action, the "conqueror" who fears that the outcome of his action will endanger the justifications which led him to become active in the first place. Wurtz's estimate is, of course, correct, but by itself too simple. The feeling we get is that while "policing" may be a necessary activity, it must be carried out without letting oneself fall into the role of the policeman. This point is well illustrated in *Les Conquérants*. The "official" inquisitioner is Nicolaieff, depicted as something of a sadist. But in an essential interrogation case, where thousands of lives are indeed at stake, Nicolaieff's methods are shown to be not only odious but incompetent as well, and it is Garine's snap decision to shoot a man in cold blood that saves the situation (see LC, pp. 154-58).

In *L'Espoir* the tables are completely turned; it is an unmistakable "enemy," a captured Italian Fascist pilot, who must be interrogated by a thoroughly likeable protagonist, Scali, chosen for the task because he speaks Italian. Scali anticipates the ordeal uneasily. Malraux neutralizes the scene to a considerable extent by applying irony to the interrogator himself. The prisoner is somewhat taken aback by this man: "What astonished him was perhaps Scali himself: this look of an American comedian, due less to his face with its heavy mouth, but with regular features despite the horn-rimmed glasses, than to his legs, too short for his body, which made him walk like Charlie Chaplin" (LE, p. 549). Scali immediately separates himself from his role: " 'Just a minute,' said Scali in Italian. 'I am not a policeman. I am a volunteer aviator' " (LE, p. 549). He does not understand a detail about Italian planes: "Let the police figure it out" (LE, p. 550). Among the personal effects of the prisoner, Scali finds a photographed detail of a fresco by Piero della Francesca, and he reflects: "Without Fascism, this man might well have been his student" (LE, p. 550). The Fascist shouts that he will be unjustly executed; Scali replies: " 'You will not be shot at all,' he said, suddenly adopting the tone of a professor scolding his student" (LE, p. 551).

The scene has no images of the theatrical; Scali consciously refuses to play the role of the interrogator (although subconsciously he comes close to being enticed by it: "Scali sensed with violence the superiority that the knowledge of lying gives over the person who is lying" [LE, p. 550]). But as in other interrogation scenes there are present the kinds of images that intrude ironically upon a serious confrontation, in this case calling into question the validity of the whole notion of who the enemy is supposed to be. And although there is no sense of shame here, we do find the expression of a shock at the end of the episode, this time applied to the interrogator as he identifies with the other and wonders how he would have been treated by the Fascists if *he* were the one being interrogated. Behind the prisoner, on a table, lies a great pile of assorted silver objects seized by anti-Fascist forces; and buried beneath this "tragic bric-a-brac," these "Aladdin's treasures," a clock begins to strike.

> These clocks (wound up for how long?) which, in the midst of this interview, so far from those who had owned them, struck some hour or other, gave Scali a strange impression of indifference and eternity; everything he said, everything he could say seemed so vain to him that all he wanted now was to stop talking. This man and he had made their choices. (LE, p. 553)

Once again, a confrontation by interrogation is depicted as a painful ordeal of humiliation and futility, in which the images dramatize an intense feeling of unreality all the while obliging the character to justify his own action to himself.

Thus far we have considered the kinds of confrontations which work upon the state of a character's mind. There are numerous instances as well of situations in which a human *act* is directly affected. All of Malraux's novels convey the general notion of a struggle between a given reality and man's capacity to influence or alter that reality. At the level of immediate confrontation this notion is frequently communicated in terms of nonhuman phenomena which seem to become animated forces, impenetrable mysteries hostile to man's desire to impose himself.

In one such pattern, phenomena seem to actively refuse being influenced by men's actions. The *Shan-Tung*, for example, a steamer bearing the arms that Katow's party must steal for their own cause, seems to play a deliberate game of evading the approach of the insurgents' boat: "The current, which was powerful at this hour, caught it crosswise; the steamer, very high now (they were directly below) seemed to take off at full speed into the night like a ghost ship" (CH, p. 232). Here resistance lasts but a few moments before the men accomplish what they set out to do. But there are instances of prolonged resistance as well. In *L'Espoir*, Attignies, in a state of semi-shock as a result of his plane crash, will swim, walk, and ride through several pages of frustrating obstacles before attaining his desired goal; and these pages are filled with incongruous figures that intrude as though to hide victory behind a veil of deceptive illusions: men seem to be playing bugles when they are actually eating, peasants wear "Mexican" blankets, the passage through a tunnel becomes a fall into a strange dream world of floating in water, a visit to a farmhouse turns up the puzzling decor of "Moorish crockery and false romantic frescoes with parrots," and even a murder occurs from which the assassin returns "as if he had come out of a stage wing, a red saber in his hand" (LE, pp. 795-800). And as though a crash landing were not a fate ironic enough for a pilot, the long awaited goal of action here is nothing more than safe arrival at a hospital, ultimately a defensive position from which the men can recover from the insistent blows of misfortune. And once again we must witness a man contemplating with disbelief the defeat of man: "The immobile heaviness of the electricity gave the whole room an unreal look; its great white unity might have been that of a dream if bloodstains and a few bodies had not savagely imposed the presence of life. . . . The room was filling with the brotherhood of the shipwrecked" (LE, p. 800).

In numerous instances the intrusion of an incongruous figure seems to question the tactics that men apply against a given reality. It is the image of the theatrical that most consistently serves this purpose, but there are others as well, helping to convey the two related attributes Malraux associates with a "romantic" attitude: a glamorous facade and a lack of discipline, both inadequate tools with which to confront the aggressive encroachment of reality. We have already seen a number of examples from *L'Espoir* which suggest strongly that a victory achieved through such a stance is a mere illusion. The most impressive instance is probably the episode in Toledo which terminates with the apparent victory of the anti-Fascist forces. What the journalist Shade senses for us sets up the two poles of contrast: on the one hand, a "mysterious unreality," with recollections of an Indian decor including "garnet palaces invaded by coconut palms," peacocks and monkeys that listen to the radio, and visions of a lunar landscape; on the other, the smells of burning and of rotting cadavers. The area around the Alcazar will turn into sheer decor, illuminated by theater projectors; an anarchist appears wearing a Mexican hat, the attendant crowds turn into Sunday strollers; and finally Hernandez will have fulfilled what Garcia calls his "personal Apocalypse": "The most dangerous thing in these half-Christians, is their taste for suffering: they are ready to commit the worst mistakes, provided they pay for them with their lives" (LE, p. 609).

Hernandez thus shares at least one major trait in common with the terrorist heroes Hong and Tchen, and with a number of minor personages who fall into the general category of "romantic" men. What they do can be called action, but it is badly conceived action, ineffective against the hard core of reality and ultimately destructive to the self. This helps explain why several of the major protagonists so strenuously reject the notion that they are identical with their legendary biographies—that is, in the sense that they are nothing more than the sum of their past romantic actions. Claude Vannec, for example, sees in Perken "this man indifferent to the pleasure of playing out his biography, detached from the need to admire his acts" (VR, p. 24). One of the implications is that an overawareness of one's own legend is an enticement to the cultivation of the self, an invitation for playing one's own theatrical role, thus thwarting an effective action outward upon reality. Perken compares his kind of action in Siam with that of his romantic predecessor thus: "I have attempted seriously what Mayrena wanted to attempt by believing he was on the stage of your theaters. To be king is idiotic; what counts is to create a kingdom. I haven't played the fool with a saber; I've hardly used my rifle" (VR, p. 86).

If the scenes of interrogation, considered above, seem so painful, it is in part due to the fact that Malraux's man resents having to give an account of himself in terms of his legend, as though that were all he were. When Walter Berger tells Vincent, plagued by men eager to read into his present and past actions that man is nothing but a "miserable little pile of secrets," Vincent will retort angrily: "A man is what he does!" (NA, p. 90)—"what he *does*," and not what he *has done*. One can hardly say that Malraux's heroes are not "glamorous"—Malraux exploits all manners of dramatic ploys to make them eminently romantic before our very eyes. But there is a clear distinction to be made between the stylistic technique of dramatizing significant experiences, and a weakness in man that entices him to apply a fossilized image of himself against an ever-changing reality that must be confronted with fresh, well-disciplined tactics. The only truly valid hero for Malraux is the eternal "conqueror," whose awareness of his own mythic aura is forever ironic.

But if romantic tactics are ineffective against reality, the anguishing fact remains that there is no proof whatsoever that serious tactics can secure a victory either, or at least not a victory in the sense of a satisfactory fulfillment of an entire program of action which can then be enjoyed by the victor. In the very midst of a serious enterprise, as we have seen in innumerable instances, the incongruous image can convey an anxious feeling of the futility of action, and actually forebode an eventual defeat. That is what happens, for example, when Jaime goes on his last bombing mission or when Kyo reaches Hankow to receive Vologuine's news. The unreal decor that dominates this latter episode, however, is a relatively minor clue compared to the overwhelming presence of Clappique. By the time Clappique comes out of the gambling room of the *Black Cat* nightclub, the fate of Kyo and of the Revolution has been determined, and the passage that follows merely recapitulates what is already well understood. Clappique steps out into the night air of Shanghai and we experience with him one of the novel's most prolonged transformations of reality into a dream decor; and as in the Toledo episode of *L'Espoir*, the two poles are again an eerie lunar landscape and the overpowering odor of death transported by the wind (CH, pp. 361-62).

Malraux seems to structure resistance into the very core of action as though to hold off single victories, and through a cumulative effect, within each novel and from one novel to the next, effectively puts into doubt whether a final victory is even possible. Geoffrey Hartman's assessment of the "obstacle-course" type of plot[6] in Malraux seems to hold for all the novels, if we include under the general notion of "obstacles," in addition to that patent manipulation of plot by which hard-earned victories are swiftly followed by the appearance of fresh dragons, such varying devices as presages of doom, intimations of the absurdity of action, the transformations of real scenes into dream decor, the unexpected reversal of events—in short, all the effects achieved through the presence of incongruous imagery.

Notes

1. Among the numerous studies on Malraux's concept of art and his art criticism, two are particularly valuable for relating art specifically to the novels: William Righter, *The Rhetorical Hero* (London: Routledge and Kegan Paul, 1964), and Pascal Sabourin, *La Réflexion sur l'art d'André Malraux* (Paris: Klincksieck, 1972).

2. Cf. Brian T. Fitch's study of alienation in Malraux in *Le Sentiment d'étrangeté chez Malraux, Sartre, Camus et S. de Beauvoir* (Paris: Minard, 1964).

3. Brian Fitch has noted the presence of the phosphorescent image as well in Malraux's early piece, *Royaume farfelu*, in "The Imagery of Malraux's *Royaume*

farfelu and its significance for the Novels," *Mélanges Malraux Miscellany* 2, no. 2 (Autumn 1970): 20-29.

4. For literal references to the experience of grandfathers with passing circuses, see VR, p. 28, CH, pp. 198-99, NA, p. 42.

5. The next sentence reads as follows: "All these wounded were soldiers: there was no panic, but a grim order, made of fatigue, impotence, rage, and determination." As is frequently the case, Malraux's expository dramatization of the heroic virtues of the people offers information that strains logic, and is notably less effective in its expressiveness than his imagistic style.

6. Geoffrey Hartman, *André Malraux* (London: Bowes and Bowes, 1960), p. 63.

Conclusion

Our consideration of Malraux's choice of analogical vehicles has shown that the author draws from a wide variety of sources. In only a few cases is there significant indication of a specialist's knowledge, notably such areas as art, anthropology and, to some extent, the cinema; the greater number of images belong to the universal realm of experience of literate Western readers. But beyond the particular questions of the content, form, or even originality of the images—all the details which have been discussed throughout this study—it may reasonably be expected that an author's particular vision of reality can be derived from studying the total body of imagery in his work. Mapping out the general terrain of that vision remains our final task.

If we consider how Malraux's images serve the decor—the material world—of his novels, it will become apparent that the effects produced through the agency of the imagery tend to fall into three major patterns. The first of these is animation and personification. Through analogy, objects that would normally be a static, phenomenal reality take on movement and attitude. Elements of the atmosphere serve as messengers of dissolution or destruction; that is, they are perceived as omens of fate. But the inanimate world can also become active agents. All manner of inanimate entities in Malraux's world assume figurative attitudes to become forces sympathetic, hostile, or indifferent to the fate of man, transforming the world into an arena of combat and destiny where man's thoughts, feelings, and acts are dramatized through the intimate participation of the cosmos.

This tendency towards animation is thus closely related to the second major pattern, the dramatization of experience. In virtually all cases where one can speak of Malraux's figurative use of decor, a powerful impulse to dramatize can be detected. Effects of light, darkness, and geometrical shapes create theatrical sets in which an experience is blown up into legendary and even mythical proportions. Images serve to render the decor of whole episodes sensuously vibrant by conveying colors, smells, noises, and qualities such as heaviness, lightness, depth, and fragility in such a way that they penetrate the consciousness of the character, and the reader, generally as a profoundly anxious perception of the world as predicament.[1]

We know from reading the novels that Malraux's characters find words a consummately inferior means of communicating among men. But the dramatic stance by which a character projects his sense of life is immensely communicable, and it is through this stance that Malraux's indispensable witness of the character's ordeal—be it another character or the reader—partakes of his experience. William Righter writes of Malraux's characters:

> The act exists in order to give meaning to human experience, and yet it is an arbitrary meaning ; in most cases its validity derives not from the fact of the action but from certain qualities of the actor himself. The act, for Malraux, in effect has meaning in so far as it is *expressive* of some essential element of our humanity—even perhaps, in so far as it has *style.* The act, therefore, depends, even in the earliest novels, on values that are to some extent aesthetic. It is expressiveness that gives dignity, or pathos or power.[2]

Malraux's character is an "actor" in both senses of the word simultaneously: he who performs actions and he who performs a dramatic role. The role dramatizes the act; without drama, and the highlighting provided by so much of the imagery, the validity of the act tends to fall out of view. This notion can also help to explain Malraux's tendency to create visual tableaux. It is a way of freezing action, to establish an esthetic distance in order to frame it, and thus dramatize its significance.

In a third major pattern, imagery which elaborates decor creates ironic effects by transforming a real setting into an unreal one. In some instances, dreamlike barriers intervene between the observer and the object of his perception to convey a sense of shock and estrangement. In other instances, a solid encounter with the real is relegated to the comic or the inauthentic, while in still others serious human activity is transformed into surface decor to serve as a corrective brake upon the swollen dimensions of the characters' will to impose their acts upon the world, just as an "indifferent" nature corrects the optimistic vision of a human-oriented cosmos.

Turning now to the manner in which the images serve characterization, we are faced with another sort of problem. If we were forced to apply the yardstick of convincing individualization to measure Malraux's success in fully rounding out his characters, we would have to conclude that the characters as a rule suffer from the author's tendency to create according to preconceived molds. The characters do not evolve much in the course of each novel (a major exception is Manuel in *L'Espoir*). Literal descriptions and introspective discourse, by themselves, come dangerously close at times to creating fragments of one complex personality, presumably that of the author himself. Malraux's technique seems to be based on varying the characters' background experiences and the direction in which psychological depth is probed—but it is to a large extent the service of the imagery that prevents the characters from resembling each other too much.

Images that describe physical traits are plentiful, but on

the whole fail to individualize the characters with great precision. A number of different kinds of analogies establish facial traits and the total aspect of a person. Quite a large number of them rely on simple human prototypes: races, nationalities, professions, the military, the clerical, and so forth. A few descriptions achieve a certain individual distinction by reference to specific historical, mythical, cinematic, and literary figures, and especially to specific works of art; but even in these cases, the physical impression is not always elaborated and, with few exceptions, notably in *Les Noyers de l'Altenburg*, remains simply a physical impression.

That the lack of individualization is not so much a failure of talent as it is a relative lack of concern on Malraux's part becomes apparent when we consider the role of other images that characterize. Images that depict moral traits do so on a universal basis, not on an individual one. Inhuman and subhuman characteristics are depicted by reference to animals and insects (in the earlier novels the crowd is most often described in terms of animal imagery), unction by reference to clerical figures, innocence and naiveté to children, childhood, and adolescence, demeaning aspects to demeaning jobs (especially kitchen jobs), a willingness to work hard to peasants, etc. Malraux's characterizations thus tend to be achieved through the accumulation of a certain number of essential human traits, while greater psychological depth is hidden in shadows beneath a public, legendary surface, reaching ultimately, at the deepest level, to universal human anxiety.

An extensive body of imagery serves to characterize human movements and gestures. Images appear with particular frequency in connection with scenes of dispersal and flight, in which Malraux seems to underscore the frailty of the human condition on a massive scale. In scenes of mass meetings, what is depicted is usually a stylized sort of regimentation, through analogy to such things as the reactions of a theater or church audience, animal motions, the regularity of machines, and so forth. In scenes of human suffering Malraux conveys a sense of anxiety and shock through various kinds of incongruous imagery.

The final major service which the imagery performs for the novels is that of supporting and concretizing a number of Malraux's themes. The prevalent vision of reality that emerges from them centers on a variety of physical and metaphysical predicaments and the character's reactions to them. The struggle between the two great powers, an inhuman fate and the human will, takes on a variety of figurative forms. Insects flying about lights, sacrifices made to figurative gods, turning in circles, finding communion with the night, the possibility of being likened to animals, of losing one's humanity to become subhuman, a savage or a machine—all these elucidate varieties of submission to fate. The predicament itself is most often embodied as a kind of imprisonment (literal and figurative), which in turn may be supported by a wide variety of vehicles. Opposed to submission is the hero's will to control the direction of his life, depicted by a movement of the hands, the straight line, leaving a "scar" on the earth, erotic sensations experienced in moments of danger, and so forth. Gambling, in the early novels, portrays an almost pathological will to conquer; that this ambition most often collapses is evidenced by an abundant body of imagery that depicts a loss of control to a higher power: figurative blindness, madness, burial, intoxication, illness, sick children, cadavers—all these point to a surrender in what appears a hopeless struggle.

Continued loss in this battle of the wills leads to an experience of humiliation, a theme which is conveyed by such imagery as the woman's role in the sex act, insects associated with imprisonment, animals associated with degradation, and so forth. Losing the battle means an ephemeral existence—in the language of imagery this is expressed, calmly in moments of reflection, as a world that turns into dust, leaves that whirl, clouds absorbed into a blank sky;

violently in moments of frustration, as disintegration, leprosy, poison. We find a vast category of images that give substance to a variety of anguished reactions depicting the human condition: internal uneasiness, claustrophobia, terror, physical pain. Material correlatives abound for expressing nervous anxieties: figurative bathing rooms, heat (literal as well as figurative), saturation, crushing, respiration, madness, the death agony, suspended time, doctors' reports to their dying patients, violent torture and execution, the heart-rending songs of Oriental chanters.

The predicament of the strong-minded hero is further compounded by an inability to break through the barrier of his ego to communicate with others. In the earlier novels we find men who are even estranged from themselves: Garine, Perken, and Ferral speak figuratively of discarded corpses, Kyo of a tonsillectomy. Alienation from the major body of society is expressed in terms of amputation, madness, sleep, death, extraterrestrial bodies. But from the very first novel on an element of hope through communication with others is introduced through the image of the child, and increasingly through the theme of manly brotherhood itself. This hope is supported by additional imagery relating to death and rebirth, apocalypse and germination, latent nobility through epic song, eternity through renewed vegetation—and in the last novel, by imagery that spans all of human time to terminate in an explosion of figures which unite Biblical and legendary marvels to an eternal present.

Malraux's world is not of the sort that can be reduced to simple, well-proportioned explanations. Men, their actions, feelings, and ideas, and the world of animate and inanimate nature are bound into one great complex force suffering from a tragic and profound internal dissension. It is a world filled with anguish and escapes from anguish, violence, defeat, and death; it is also a world of rebellion, hope in triumph, latent human grandeur striving to find an appropriate expression and a will to awareness at all costs. The function of Malraux' images is precisely that of projecting a series of multiple perspectives upon reality, so that its every aspect is mirrored against every other aspect, to be refracted finally against the membrane of a single consciousness, that of the author himself. The images are, in short, an indispensable tool for expanding and ordering the experience out of which are finally born the novels.

Notes

1. Cf. my remarks on Malraux's dramatization of the act of perception itself, "Ironic Figures in Malraux's Novels," in W. M. Frohock, ed., *Image and Theme: Studies in Modern French Fiction* (Cambridge, Mass.: Harvard University Press, 1969), pp. 38-44.
2. *The Rhetorical Hero* (London: Routledge and Kegan Paul, 1964), pp. 8-9.

Bibliography

Works by André Malraux:

Antimémoires. Paris: Gallimard, 1967.

Romans (Les Conquérants, La Condition humaine, L'Espoir). Bibliothèque de la Pléiade. Paris: Gallimard, 1947.

Les Noyers de l'Altenburg. Paris: Gallimard, 1948.

Le Temps du mépris. Paris: Gallimard, 1935.

La Voie Royale. Paris: Gallimard, 1930.

Critical Works:

Blumenthal, Gerda. *André Malraux: The Conquest of Dread.* Baltimore, Md.: Johns Hopkins University Press, 1960.

Carduner, Jean. *La Création romanesque chez Malraux.* Paris: Nizet, 1968.

Ellis, Elizabeth, A. "André Malraux et le monde de la nature." *Archive des Lettres Modernes*, no. 157 (1975).

Falk, Eugene H. *Types of Thematic Structure: The Nature and Function of Motifs in Gide, Camus and Sartre.* Chicago: University of Chicago Press, 1967.

Fitch, Brian T. "The Imagery of Malraux's *Royaume farfelu* and its Significance for the Novels." *Mélanges Malraux Miscellany* 2, no. 2 (Autumn 1970): 20-29.

______. *Le Sentiment d'étrangeté chez Malraux, Sartre, Camus et S. de Beauvoir.* Paris: Minard, 1964.

Frank, Joseph. *The Widening Gyre.* New Brunswick, N.J.: Rutgers University Press, 1963.

Frohock, W. M., ed. *Image and Theme: Studies in Modern French Fiction.* Cambridge, Mass.: Harvard University Press, 1969.

______. "Notes on Malraux's Symbols." *Romanic Review* 42 (December 1951): 274-81.

Girard, René. "Le Règne animal dans les romans d'André Malraux." *French Review* 26 (1953): 261-67.

Hartman, Geoffrey. *André Malraux*. London: Bowes and Bowes, 1960.

Horvath, Violet M. *André Malraux: The Human Adventure*. New York: New York University Press, 1969.

Kline, Thomas J. *André Malraux and the Metamorphosis of Death*. New York: Columbia University Press, 1973.

Nichols, James C. "Malraux's Use of Sexual Metaphor in *La Voie Royale*." *Mélanges Malraux Miscellany* 6, no. 1 (Spring 1974): 4-14.

Rees, G. O. "Animal Images in the Novels of André Malraux." *French Studies* 9 (1955): 129-42.

Righter, William. *The Rhetorical Hero*. London: Routledge and Kegan Paul, 1964.

Robbins, Kittye Delle. "Legends of Good Women: Medieval Images in the Novels of André Malraux." *Mélanges Malraux Miscellany* 5, no. 2 (Autumn 1973): 3-8.

Sabourin, Pascal. *La Réflexion sur l'art d'André Malraux*. Paris: Klincksieck, 1972.

Sonnenfeld, Albert. "Malraux and the Tyranny of Time: The Circle and the Gesture." *Romanic Review* 54 (October 1963): 198-212.

Tarica, Ralph. "Ironic Figures in Malraux's Novels." In *Image and Theme: Studies in Modern French Fiction*, edited by W. M. Frohock. Cambridge, Mass.: Harvard University Press, 1969.

Thompson, Brian. "The Image of Blindness in Malraux's Meditations on Art." *Mélanges Malraux Miscellany* 3, no. 2 (Autumn 1971): 16-25.

Ullmann, Stephen. *Style in the French Novel*. Cambridge: at the University Press, 1957.

Index

Names of characters in Malraux's novels are followed in parentheses by the standard abbreviation of the novel in which they are found